An Ordinary, But A Little Extraordinary Life

An Ordinary, But A Little Extraordinary Life

LEE'S STORY

JB Yanni

JB Yanni

For Mom,
Who always was, and will always be, my greatest hero

Contents

One

Introduction

Nearly ten years ago, my mother was diagnosed with Alzheimer's. This news put my entire family on a reading mission. We read every news story, book and article we could find. In that search, we found several books that were very personal stories. Everything I read was an insight into the enormous impact of this disease. They were tales of loss. Loss of control, loss of memories, loss of all things that made up some person now suffering from Alzheimer's. Well worth the read, but heartbreaking, and you must read them with a box of Kleenex handy. The degenerative nature of Alzheimer's culminates in that one horrific moment when that loved one no longer recognizes their own family, and these stories chronical that journey in a very relatable, but often painful manner.

What I find sorely lacking from this array of touching and helpful material is something I came to realize over many moments with my mother, and culminating in one very sunny day in October a little more than a year ago. The story missing from the vast array of material on Alzheimer's is the celebration of the life lived, both before the diagnosis and afterward. The story of the remarkable person who is on the verge of being lost forever. What made them laugh, made them cry, and made them who they are. I've met many people since my mother's diagnosis. They all had moments to share, moments of someone dear to them.

Despite that, there seemed to be no story out there that celebrated the life of a person facing Alzheimer's. This may be because I have yet to find such a book, but I find it heartbreaking that with all the people suffering from Alzheimer's, there is not a library full of books celebrating and chronicling the lives of these people. Not just to honor those suffering, but to provide the families and those that surround these patients with a means to heal and remember.

What is most tragic to me, as a daughter, and a writer, is how little by little, I'm losing my mother and with her, all the memories she held of her life and our lives. This horrific disease that neither disfigures nor eats away at someone physically, but so painfully takes a person's memories, experiences and relationships from them. Along the way, it takes someone dear from those who shared the life of that patient. Not suddenly, but inch by inch, day by day, over an extended time.

As the immortal Toni Morrison once said, "If you can't find the story you want to read, you should write it." So, here it is. It is a celebration for every patient, every caregiver, every family member, to the life well lived. It is a tribute to the often-ordinary nature of most of our lives, but in retrospect, the heroic people that walk around us each day, that touch us with their laughter, their love and their unending strength.

This is a story for and about my mother. A woman born in 1940 in a small town in central Illinois. She has two younger sisters. Raised primarily by their mother, after the sudden and traumatic death of their father. My mother is not a celebrity. She is not renowned for any significant accomplishment. You will not find my mother gracing the cover of any magazine, nor is she documented outside of her yearbooks. She played in the band, married her high school sweetheart, raised four children, and enjoyed a loving family and a wide set of friends. My mother baked, babysat grandchildren, and built dollhouses. She was a nurse, a mother, a cashier, and a real estate agent. Yes, it is an ordinary life, you might say, but you would be wrong. To call her life ordinary would miss the truly extraordinary woman who is my mother. The little girl that trampled the garden happily with her friend, voted most popular of her senior class, while getting chased around by her mother for talking back, was full of mischief, love, strength and devotion.

She is wrapped up in literally every memory I have. The good, the great, the bad and the ugly, she is there with me. She has been the sounding board for every major decision of my life. Present for every art show, track meet, and award ceremony; nearby for the birth of my children, and the shoulder I cried on when I had my many miscarriages. She has been my counselor, and she is the example by which I judge myself as a mother, a wife and a person.

As I have talked to her friends, family and classmates, and learned all these bits and moments of her life, I have learned that she is, and was, so much more than the mom that nursed me through tonsillitis and broken hearts. She was carefree and fun-loving and had a great sense of humor. And while she was strong enough to wrestle four children through the department store to prepare for a new school year, she dreamed many dreams and played pranks, had fun and got in trouble.

Alzheimer's has the power to reduce a loved one to something barely recognizable, but it cannot and will not erase the vibrant and loving life of my mother. In that, the disease has already failed. It may ultimately take my mother from those who love her, but we will overcome because we have these memories of this loving, beautiful woman and her legacy, of her life, her gifts and her spirit to carry with us for generations to come. This is the celebration of her ordinary, and maybe a little extraordinary life.

Two

The Fateful Day

Although she was diagnosed years ago, and one could say the fateful day was that day when we learned she had Alzheimer's, the truly fateful day for me came last October. My mother's disease started as many Alzheimer's patients start. She couldn't remember that she asked about something, so she asked again, and again. She got a bit lost one day returning home from a luncheon with women she knew, which was about when we discouraged her driving herself anywhere. She forgot things you told her. It was funny at first, then a bit trying, and I think the diagnosis helped us all focus and work together to provide her the best care and maintain the best quality of life. For me, the diagnosis was the moment I found my patience, and realized that the tables had turned, and it was now time for the children to help the parents. As a younger person, I always imagined this moment and wondered when it might happen. Would we, myself and my siblings, be ready? Would we be at a place in our own lives where we could manage it? At no point has it felt like an obligation, however. Helping my mother and father has seemed not like a repayment, but a tribute to what they gave me and my siblings, and who we are. I would like to say I felt totally prepared, but that wouldn't be true. If truth be told, I doubt anyone is truly prepared to shift their focus to care for parents.

The Alzheimer's advanced, as it does. She'd see something or hear something and try to tie events and people together that were separated by years or circumstances. Once, while travelling back and forth to Florida, having stopped for lunch, she asked when a real estate colleague was joining us, and when I said he wasn't, she insisted for nearly fifteen minutes we had to wait for him. I've never understood what about that day, the restaurant or the circumstances brought that stop for lunch together with a former colleague. She became very protective of her things and got almost hostile if she thought something was missing. If it was missing, it likely was because she had decided to put it away, and it took us weeks to locate it, underneath something else, in a drawer where it had never been kept before. Then she got a little belligerent and swore. Surprisingly, that seemed to settle down when we began labelling the cabinets and closets with the contents found inside. However, for about a year I threatened to embroider two pillows for her. One that said "In a minute" and one that said "Bullshit", as those had become her two favorite responses to any question or comment. Do you need to go to the bathroom I would ask, "In a minute" she would reply, and her response to anything that she didn't like in that moment was "Bullshit."

Then she began pounding her hands on the arms of chairs and tables all of a sudden. When you asked her what was the matter, she would occasionally say she didn't like this. Clearly, she had some awareness that she was losing her memories, I thought, but when asked, she could not define or explain what "this" meant to her. It got harder and harder for her to manage the transition between my parent's summer home in Chicago and their winter home in Florida. Eventually, Dad realized they had to have only one home. Dad gave up a lot. He was helping to coach the area football team. But Mom couldn't be left alone. My youngest sister, Jan and I would take turns sitting with her during football games, taking her to dinner and shopping. Even that became too hard and he decided to give it up. Our father would travel around to watch grandchildren at their track meets, football games, golf tournaments and wrestling matches. He had to stop doing that too. Probably too late, his children realized the depth of his devotion to his wife. It is clear to me every day now. The depth of their devotion to one another has been evident throughout my life on some level, it just seemed more one-sided for many years with my father carrying the burden of supporting our family, while my mother carried almost everything else. Now, their roles have reversed. He carries the burden of absolutely everything.

Any one of those points in the progression of her disease could be considered fateful days. Perhaps they all were. It was difficult, in those moments when I would look into my mother's eyes and know that the person I knew was momentarily gone. The first few times it happened, I was surprised and overcome with sadness, but I kept convincing myself that we could manage this disease and if we could just keep her in stage one longer, it would be ok. It was a game I would play with myself. If she had a particularly good day, I would presume they would keep happening, even when the good days, in fact, didn't go on, and were not consistent. I was fooling myself, I guess. This little game is what led to my fateful day.

My parents had permanently lived in Florida for nearly a year by last year. During that year, Rich, my husband, and I made several trips to visit them. These trips served several purposes for me. One, they helped assuage my guilt over not being close enough to just run over at any point to help out. My being twenty hours away was proving more difficult than I had first imagined and at least once every day I felt guilty about not being there to help in her care. Two, it allowed me to be there for my father. He is her primary caregiver and unless you've been in that position, or witnessed this, you have no idea how hard that can be. Any time he gets to go unwind in his office, nap in his chair, or go out to run errands and not have to worry about keeping a watchful eye on her, is a relief, I'm sure. But also, it is necessary for his sanity to get away from that constant responsibility for her safety. Finally, and I'm not ashamed to admit this, going to my parent's house is a salve for my soul. They don't have to do or say anything, just being where they live is a fortifying comfort. Truthfully, if I'm honest with myself, that last reason is usually the first in my mind when planning these trips because these visits tend to coincide with moments in my life when I need just that fortification.

It's funny, but every time I went home, since starting college, I have felt that surge of strength pour into my soul when I came through their door. It always reminds me of a time my freshman year of college when I was suffering from every cold that passed near me and just wanted to go home for the weekend. I wanted my mother to make me chicken soup and put another blanket on my while I laid on the couch. I finally found a ride and called home to ask to be picked up at Oakbrook Mall, about twenty-five minutes from our home. Of course, my mother said she would, but she added that everyone had all kinds of plans for the weekend and she doubted she would be able to take care of me. I smiled when she said it, and replied, it was fine, I just needed to be home. As I recall she didn't really respond to that comment, and may not have understood what I meant. I think of that weekend every time I arrive at their house.

But back to that day. Rich, and I came for a week-long visit and mid-way through the visit, Mom started having all kinds of issues. She was incoherent, and couldn't pick her feet up when she walked. She seemed very disoriented, like she did when she didn't sleep enough. When she began to stumble and not be able to stand up, we decided to take her to the emergency room. Here's the thing about hospitals, my father hates them. I don't really know where it originally came from, but at this stage in their lives, I know he fears that if one of them goes into the hospital, they might not come out. Consequently, whenever we have to go there, the anxiety level escalates. Oh, and we were in the middle of a pandemic. So, there I was, with my sister, sitting on a bench outside of the ER entrance, waiting for my father to text us what was going on inside. The panic, my gosh, the panic I felt as I sat on that bench was more than I can describe. Unable to sit still, I walked across the driveway to the river and paced around the ER doorway. Mom was admitted, and while they were testing her for Covid, they also tested her for the cause of her disorientation and discovered that she had a severe urinary tract infection.

Two days later, amid confusion over which doctor was to see her, what treatment was being ordered, and lack of information being given to my father on a Saturday, he pulled my mother from the hospital. On Monday morning, we spoke to the nurse at their family doctor and were told to go immediately back to ER because of her potassium level and liver levels they discovered when reviewing bloodwork done during her stay but neither my father nor I were ever told about. Back to the hospital we went, and back to the bench I sat. We, my sisters and I, had to take turns visiting her, and for a few days we managed to sit together in the cafeteria, but eventually the security team became aware of our loitering during a pandemic and we were forced to sit outside. To say it was awful is an understatement of the highest order. My kids call me a control enthusiast. I know they're really saying I'm a control freak, and to a certain extent it's probably true. What is definitely true is that I hate, absolutely hate, feeling helpless. That's how this felt, sitting on a bench outside the entrance of the hospital. Wanting desperately to see my mother, but not wanting to make my father leave her.

Mom did get better and was about to be discharged, and Rich and I had to get back home so we left town the day after she got home. At my own home again, we tried to manage the dog, the laundry, work and my writing while checking in with Dad and my older sister, Jean, and my younger sister, Jan, every day. It lasted one week. A week later, on Saturday evening, we got a call. Mom was headed back to the hospital. I freaked out. Rich could tell I was freaking out while I was on the phone talking to Jan, or Jean. Even now I can't remember who I spoke to that night. While I talked, Rich began packing. He knew without even seeing my face, we had to go. At 9:30pm, we left the house and I drove all night, imagining the worst. I stopped once at rest stop in Georgia and tried to sleep for a few minutes. I was instantly dreaming of arriving at the hospital only to find out the worst possible thing had happened so back on the road south we went.

Mom was in Intensive Care. Dad came down so I could go visit her, because again, we were still in a pandemic and the hospital didn't care that my mother was in crisis. I hesitantly entered the ward, and her room. I stood in the doorway to her room for what seemed like an hour. I was in shock. She looked tiny in that bed, hooked up to all kinds of monitors, with a ventilator. I was in shock and I was afraid. After I went back downstairs so my father could be in the room to meet with the doctors

I sat there, numb. My mother had woken up and did recognize me, one of my many fears whenever I leave Florida, that she would not recognize me the next time. But I was still shaken to the core. I sat on the bench in front of the hospital, trembling. It was a beautiful day. The sun was shining, it was warm. You know, one of those days you wish you could just sit outside and admire nature. I was lost in my panic for some time, when, finally I looked up, and looked around. People were coming and going into and out of the hospital. Some were aided in getting into and out of their cars. Mother's brought children to see doctors, and babies were leaving with new mothers. I watched them and wondered what was going on in their lives in that moment of their day to day lives. And, I wondered if they knew what was going on with me. I wondered if they knew by the look on my face that I was suddenly very aware of the finite nature of life. I've lost family members, true, but there was something terrifying about contemplating the loss of a parent, my mother. As I sat there, I considered for really the first time, what life would be like without my mother. I was trembling in the warm sunlight.

This was the fateful day. It was the day Jean, my older sister, and I began asserting our participation in our parent's healthcare. We spoke to the family doctor, the neurologist, and the cardiologist first to ensure our mother's care. It was a day of reckoning for me. It would be completely untrue to say I got up from the bench, trembling, and was instantly ready to face the day I wouldn't have my parents with me. It wasn't the end of that battle. It was the first day of a battle I still fight to this day. However, it was a moment for me where I recognized that I could not just sit and watch it happen. I couldn't stand by while I lost my mother to Alzheimer's without knowing who she was. Without committing the memories and experiences to something that could help me begin to prepare for what is inevitably to come, and to share with others so they too could prepare.

Later that day, after Mom had been moved out of ICU, and taken off the ventilator, and I had visited her several more times, I was sitting on the couch in my parent's house and I realized that although I had heard many stories about my mother growing up, I didn't really know the person she was. I wanted to know what she was like as a little girl, what she dreamed of doing, what made her laugh before she was burdened with raising children and what her interests were before she spent all of her time being one of our cheerleaders. Before she lost all memory of her life, I wanted to gather it all together and record it. The idea of doing this became suddenly very important. I thought about reading it aloud to her, watching her face as I told her stories of her life and she remembered. That is what made this the fateful day. That is the day I started on this journey to learn more about her. It was the day I decided to write this book.

Mom on the surf board!

Three

⌒

Knocked Out Teeth, Glasses, the Trampoline and the Baptism

My mother was born on July 21, 1940. Her parents were Floye and Charles Hoyt. Mom was the oldest of three girls. I'm pretty sure my mother and her sisters are the link to why all of my siblings and I have names that start with "J", because my mother and all her sister's names start with "L". I don't know if that was the plan when my mother was born, because my mother was named for her grandfather, Lee Hoyt, but her sisters, born later, are named Linda and Lucinda. I guess it was a thing, but I don't know any other family that has this naming tradition. Growing up, my mother was Tootie, a nickname her father gave her, Linda was Lollie, probably a shortened version of her name given by some younger family member, and Lucinda was simply Cindy. Close to three years separate my mother from Linda and then there is a big gap of eight more years until Cindy was born. Because they were close in age, Linda and my mother were together all the time. My mother and her closest sister often had matching or nearly matching clothes made by my grandmother and great-grandmother for them. My great-grandmother, Myrtle (I know, strange name, but we are talking about a woman born before 1900), was a character. Among other things, she is the oldest of ten children and grew up during the depression. She was also an expert seamstress, and made much of my mother's and Linda's

Tootie and Lollie in their matching clothes

clothing, including some extravagant organdy dresses for their 8th grade graduations. Unheard of today, this was common practice in the 40's and 50's for two reasons. First, there just were not as many stores as we have today, and Amazon was nowhere to be found. Two, it was much less expense to buy material and patterns and make clothes than to buy them. My mother had nearly white blond hair when she was little. It darkened as she aged, but as a little girl she was blond. It may have been true for all the girls, but I know for sure my mother started blond. This seems strange to me, because of course, I've always known her as a brunette.

My mother and her father were very close. They used to write notes to each other when he was away for work. He had to travel on the train a couple of times a year for conventions, and when he was leaving or away for several days, he'd write her. Each Saturday, Mom and her father would travel to her private trombone lessons and spent time visiting his clients. My grandmother was an only child, but my grandfather had a brother and a sister. Lee, my mother's namesake, and my grandfather's dad, was a painter and a wall paperer. He died in the late 1940's of esophageal/ stomach cancer. My grandfather's brother and sister remained close, and my mother was very close with her cousin Gene, the son of one of those siblings of my grandfather's.

Most of these details are known to me, since I was a small child. I think most people know the basics such as these. What I was searching for was something more, something deeper.

When I decided to embark on this journey to discover who my mother was, I immediately called upon my two aunts. They frequently talked about family and people they knew from when they were younger, and I attentively listened to their stories at each visit, and during each holiday dinner. I've always been interested in what our family history is, and who my grandparents, and great grandparents were. I love looking at all the old pictures, and luckily my family keeps certificates, letters, enlistment and discharge papers and all manner of records, as well as all the old photos. I'm sure some of this comes from my interest in history in general. It's more than that though. It's a connectedness that I have always known was present with my family. As a young girl, I used to spend time at my aunts' houses, playing with my cousins, we gathered for birthdays and big events, and spent much time together. They are a big part of who I am. My aunt Linda was always decorating when I was growing up, or cleaning, or moving. She now has this amazing house that seems to ooze warmth. I love going there. It is, in fact, the second most important place to me behind only my parents' home. My aunt Cindy has always felt like my kindred spirit. She seems like the renegade of the family, which I'm sure I am too, confirmed regularly by the family stories. Being so young, I think she might have viewed her older sisters as caretakers, but I'm sure she worked hard to be grown up like her sisters, and this likely included trying to live up to their antics and I know it precipitated an early start to Cindy's smoking. She also rescued me on more than one occasion from college. She would drive over to ISU and pick me up and feed me and help me recharge on a weekend. Each year, Cindy has an amazing garden on her farm and although I promised to never tell, sucked her thumb into adulthood. Now that my mother is becoming more and more affected by Alzheimer's, my aunts have in some respects taken on the role my mother had as my sounding board. Checking in with them, particularly on writing projects has become mandatory for me. So, not unlike going home, their homes have also proved to be a huge comfort to me.

On one of those visits to Linda's house, I was sitting at Linda's kitchen table, with a box or two of pictures at the center between us, listening to the stories of the little girl my mother was. It was shocking to learn that my mother and her side-kick younger sister were both ingenious and sneaky. To say Tootie and Lollie were cohorts would miss the fact that it was often unclear who was the instigator and who was the follower of their antics. It thrills me when I consider their adventures, because I know I would have been right there with them, and I love the fact that my mother had a feisty side.

Nowadays, we don't really wax floors. Basketball courts maybe, but generally not our household floors. I don't mean Swiffer cleaning here. I'm talking about down on your knees scrubbing floors and then applying a wax to the floor with a mop or brush and it made the floor very slick. Back in the 1940's this was a regular practice. Just after one such waxing, my mother and her sister were sliding across the kitchen floor, probably trying to see who could slide the farthest, when my mother, obviously the winner of this competition, slid all the way into the kitchen and hit a chair, knocking out her two front teeth. Luckily these were baby teeth, but still. I laughed when I heard this, and went hunting through the pictures as Linda was telling this wild tale to see if I could find one of my mother, with the missing front teeth. There are none, I am assured because my mother wouldn't really show her gaping grin until her adult teeth came in. I can clearly remember my mother admonishing me for doing this very thing two or three decades after she perfected the move, although our clean floors were probably never this slick. Apparently, what is good for the goose, is not so good for the gander! Linda laughs as she tells me this, and we sit for a minute, pondering this little girl slamming into a chair. I wonder if she got extra money from the tooth fairy for the sudden loss...

Tootie and Lollie in their front yards - plotting something!

Each year, my mother and her sister would visit the doctor and assess their eyesight. We all do this, and as one who has worn glasses since the fourth grade, I understand that each year, you want something new, and usually have to pick out a new pair of glasses. Most of the time this is because your eyesight has changed, but we know, everyone really wants something new. You've grown a year older, your tastes change, and your glasses should change too. One such year, my mother was told she didn't need a new prescription and she could just keep wearing the same glasses for another year, while Linda got to pick out a new pair. This was disappointing to my mother and to the two of them, seemed wholly unfair. Later that day, while the two girls were discussing this, and lamenting at the unfair situation in which they found themselves, someone came up with a plan. Now, the storyteller would not take responsibility for this plan, and I probably can't confirm this with my mother, so who the mastermind was is lost to the years. They decided that they would spin around the divider of their two closets until they were so dizzy, they fell, thereby, and hopefully, breaking my mother's glasses so that she would have to have a new pair. No telling how many bruises they acquired in enacting the plan, but after not succeeding, they resorted to simply stomping on the glasses. Truthfully, I had my doubts about this dizzy circling ever resulting in the glasses braking, but nevertheless, I commend them on the logic and enthusiasm. The glasses were broken and my mother did get a new pair. If their parents were ever aware of the cause of the broken glasses, they never told. I wonder, if perhaps Grandma Floye knew, and just didn't say a word. She was that kind of grandmother. Perhaps she wasn't the same as a mother, but it's fun to think of her laughing with my grandfather about the ingenious plan to force the purchase of the new glasses. As I think of this, I imagine what she'd say and smile. Grandma Floye has always spoken her mind!

Several years later, after Cindy was born, and my mother was old enough, my grandparents decided to leave their two daughters, Lee and Linda, in charge to watch their younger sister so the parents could conduct a shopping trip in some peace. That same week, the school had procured a new fantastic piece of equipment. They had a trampoline. As the two girls were watching their young sister, they decided that it would be a really good idea if they were prepared for the trampoline in their PE classes that week, by practicing. Cindy's crib was in their parent's room and she was happily napping. The girls were certain that watching her from their parent's room would be best, since they had been told to watch her. They figured watching her from the same room would be just what their parents wanted. They were also certain that practicing jumping on their parent's bed was the best way to prepare for the trampoline at school. Following the directions of their parents, while doing what they really wanted, must have made them both feel they had the world by the tail. They each took a turn and then decided to jump together. It was at this point, the wooden supports, called slats, holding the springs and mattress up above the frame of the bed, broke. The bed fell down, inside the frame to the floor. Hoping to disguise their activity, they straightened the bed, and covers and left the room. Imagine for a minute, the springs and mattress well below the sides of the frame with covers neatly straightened. Naturally, when their parents returned, one of them went to check on Cindy, peacefully sleeping in her crib, and discovered the bed, now resting on the floor, inside the frame of the bed. Questions were asked, I'm sure. I never knew my grandfather. He died long before I was born. But I know that he was very close with his oldest daughter. And I have seen him in photos looking at my mother as a baby and child in a devoted manner, so I doubt he was too harsh with them. Who knows? My own parents were strict in terms of the rules of the house, so I suspect their parents were too. This type of behavior when I was thirteen or fourteen years old would have found me grounded to my room or the house for some extended period of time. The lumber yard was, of course closed, as it was after noon on Saturday. Remember, it was in the 1940s and 50s, and stores did not remain open all day on Saturday and were never open on Sundays. My Grandfather did, thankfully, know how to reach the owner of the lumber yard and called him, described the situation, and convinced the man to open long enough for my grandfather to get the two by fours to repair his bed. It would have been interesting to hear that conversation, what the two men's assessment of the first babysitting day was.

Hearing people's conversations was possible back then as most people had a party line. In addition, being so long ago, there were operators that performed a function of connecting you to the number you wanted to reach. For those of you unfamiliar with this concept, houses had telephones wired to the wall. They usually were mounted on the wall, in fact. In small communities, the infrastructure was such that you would share a "line" with the neighbors. If you picked up the operator would ask for the number. Of course, private lines were available for a higher cost. In fact, my great-grandparents had a private line as my great-grandfather was a doctor. My grandparents also had a private line, because my grandfather was the fire chief. Oh, and the numbers were very short. Interestingly, the doctor's number was 334 and the fire chief's number was 443. I would have loved to hear my grandfather describe his predicament, and ask for some help. I also wouldn't mind hearing my sweet mother get hollered at for breaking a bed!

Even before then, my mother was making her feisty, smart-mouthed personality known. In 1943, on a very hot July day, Linda was being baptized. Mom was three years old. Everyone was very dressed up, standing in a church that probably did not enjoy central air-conditioning. When all was quiet during a break in the service, my mother belted out, "I'm hot! When can we go to Share Acres for a beer!"? I'm sure, despite the surroundings, some of the attendees laughed. I laughed out loud when I heard this story of my mother garnering attention and church and then told my own story about church. When my daughter was probably 4 or 5 years old, we were attending a formal Easter mass. A joyous service with bells and singing. She was sitting on the kneeler and looking at a book she had brought to keep entertained and when the music stopped, she decided to prolong the moment by beginning to sing six little ducks. The horrifying part was that several other children near us began signing with her, and the entire service was stopped for an entire chorus of six little ducks. Later the priest leaned down to me and said he thought the children's choir tryouts were later that week. Oh, to be the parent when a child does something so simple, so candid in such a moment.

I sit for a minute after hearing these stories. I can say it, my mother was a real feisty troublemaker when she was little! I love this about her. I smiled to myself as I thought I love the fact that even in the 1940's she was the kind of girl that took chances and played games and had fun. Plus, being the primary troublemaker in my family, I really love that my mother was one too. Also, as I look at the pictures Linda has given me, I've come to realize, that she too came from a home where laughter and fun in simple acts were plenty. I'm reminded of the fun my own family had when I was growing up. The little moments like when my brother asked if he could trade his baseball card collection for a brother when my youngest sister was born and he was facing a lifetime with three sisters. Or when we drove to Chillicothe in a snow storm for Christmas and the dog needed to be let out and we nearly lost him in the snow. He was white, and small and it quickly became a rescue mission when he fell down into a pile of snow! Or the games we would play in the car to keep busy during long drives, like the Alphabet game or better yet, when we would argue about space in the backseat. In case you grew up in another time than the 1970s, we had no car seats or even seatbelts in the back seats of cars then. Regular arguments erupted between us over who had the most room on the seats and imaginary lines were drawn that couldn't be crossed. These snippets of our lives keep us connected and create an unbreakable bond between us. I look around at my aunts and acknowledge this. We again, as we so often do when we are together, tell the signatory tales of each of the members of my family. My sister who still hasn't been given permission to cross Roosevelt Road, my phase of declaring that no one in my family loved me. The stories make us all laugh, and I realize they are like a warm blanket that engulfs my family.

It's also kind of amazing to come face to face with the person your mother was and realize she was just a girl once. She tried new things and came up with solutions only young children can dream up. Faced with no new glasses, she came up with the perfect plan to require new glasses, breaking the old ones! I think we would have been friends. If I was her age, and not her daughter, I like to think we would have been friends.

Four

~

The Swearing Jar, Aunt Elma, and Childhood Illness

My great grandmother is a bit of a scandal. Maybe she is scandalous only inside our family, but judgement should be reserved here. She was married, but then divorced to marry a man she was probably having an affair with. They left town in the early days of the depression and came back with a daughter, my grandmother after a few years while my great-grandfather worked for a drug company. I like to tell this story to people in a sordid kind of way with the right pauses and facial expressions. I think it's funny, that I have this scandalous woman in my family. I add that he, my great grandfather, was the town doctor, so it sounded like she was a bit of a gold digger, going after someone she thought was better and would take care of her. She did always covet the nice things others had. Oh, and this was all long before 1940. Further, my grandmother's maiden name is not my great-grandfather's name. That's the scandal part. You understand now, right? Married people didn't divorce and have affairs in the 1940s.

What I remember about her most was her long hair always up in the same bun near the top of her head. The fact that we weren't allowed to sit in her living room, but we could sit in the piano room, and we could do whatever we wanted in my great-grandfather's old office space. The office was attached to her dining room and the surprising part is that my great grandmother didn't mind our being there despite the fact that when I was little, there were medical instruments and drugs in that office still. There was a great big rolltop desk with all kinds of drawers and cubby holes. It had a chair that was on a big screw so it would swing around and around. My cousin, Janet, and I would swing that chair around until we were dizzy. I don't remember being in my great grandmother's bedroom until after she went into the nursing home. She always had liverwurst in her refrigerator and she only served desserts in enormous helpings. She lived through the depression and she hated banks, at least that's what she told me. I think surviving the depression might play into her restrictions of her living room, her bedroom, the liverwurst and the miserly way she seemed to spend money. I'm told by my aunts, my mother and grandmother that she was just mean to her daughter, my grandmother. She didn't seem mean to me, but very restrictive about her things. It probably more complicated than that, but I was a child and that's my impression. One other fact that adds to the mystery of who she was, my great grandmother swore like a sailor.

My mother and Linda seemed to spend a lot of time with their grandparents, I know this by the photos and the fact that this was part of my upbringing, spending time with grandparents. My great grandfather was called Pappy. My great grandmother was Grandma Myrt. Her name was Myrtle Thomas, his was Dr. H.V. Thomas. During the ten days my grandmother was in the hospital having Cindy, Linda and Tootie stayed with their grandparents. They vacationed with them, and spent much time at their home on 4th street. At some point, when my mother and Linda were probably in elementary school, it was decided that they would have a "stop the swearing" contest and each time a person broke the rule and swore, they had to place a quarter in the jar if they were caught. I'm sure this game was started because of my Grandma Myrt. It was probably Pappy who was trying to get her stop. He must have thought a little shaming was in order and that if her grandchildren were involved, it might change her behavior. I believe the participants were my mother, my aunt Linda, Grandma Myrt and Pappy, but it could have also included my grandparents. Grandma Myrt lost, badly, and if she was true to form in terms of her miserly spending of money, it probably hurt badly too, because of all the quarters she had to put in that jar! I like this about her though. I like that she was a scandal and swore and stored money in coffee cans. I don't like to think of how mean she was to her only daughter, but I like that she was sassy and courageous. I also like that she lost at the swearing game and was still swearing when I was a child. I'm sure that's where my mother learned all the creative words she starting using when the Alzheimer's really set in, I realize as I hear this story and finally stop laughing. It was amazing to me that a woman I had never heard swear the whole time I was growing up, could just pop off like that, but that's what my mother did for nearly a year. It feels like a long time ago now, when my mother went through that phase of the disease. Alzheimer's has robbed her even of this. She doesn't swear much anymore, in that way she is the mother I always knew. In this moment, I feel a great link connecting us all. Truth be told, I do swear, sometimes a lot. Not in front of my parents, mind you. I still can't do that, even at my age. So, despite my decorum to bite my tongue in front of my parents, I too swear a blue streak like Grandma Myrt. I guess there's just a little of the sassy Grandma Myrt in all of us!

Apparently, my Grandma Myrt is not the only character in my family. My mother and her sisters had an Aunt Elma. She's grandma Myrt's younger sister. She was married to a member of the Peacock family. C.D. Peacock is a

The glamourous Aunt Elma

jewelry store. It was founded in 1837 by Elijah Peacock. Aunt Elma was married to a younger Elijah Peacock Turner. It, in fact, was the first registered business in Chicago and the oldest existing retailer in Chicago. Aunt Elma's husband, Elijah died in an accident between a train and a car, probably before my mother was born. Aunt Elma went on to marry Deck (his last name was Decker) but he sustained a terrible head injury as a serviceman during WWII and after several surgeries, changed so much they divorced. She is always referred to in the family as being single. She and my mother became close when she lived with my great-grandparents when they returned from their years in the east.

Aunt Elma was a buyer for a Chicago drug store chain and she has been considered the glamorous member of the family for some time. She used to send my mother and Linda packages at Christmas with perfume and other fancy items. Tootie and Lollie made a bar out of the perfume bottles and mom always coveted Elma's open-toed satin slippers and fancy clothing. Later, and I'm not sure if this was when she died, or gifted throughout their lives, several C.D. Peacock pieces of china were dispersed among the family. Elma had inherited it all from two Peacock aunts, and when Grandma Myrt and Grandma Floye helped Elma clean out the house these Peacock aunts had, the china came with. Cindy had this dish that was rectangular, like a casserole pan. They used to throw their keys and change into it at the end of the day, and it sat on a hutch cabinet in their kitchen. Then, they had the dish appraised. They don't throw keys into it anymore. My mother had a collection of plates. She displayed them in the dining room of the house I grew up in on a plate rack. Back then, I wasn't terribly found of them. They were a pain to dust. I think it's pretty cool that we have this glamourous woman in our family, though. I wish I could have known her. I wish more, knowing how my mother admired her, that these memories weren't taken from her.

When I heard about this tradition of the Christmas package full of fancy bottles and things, I see it as one more courageous woman in my family. I have a vision of my mother opening this box full of treasures and I see her holding her hands up near her face, fisted, grinning and making her "Eeeeeh" sound. She does that when she's excited. I ask

Cindy and Linda if she did that when she was young. Yes, she did. I smile, thinking of the other times she's done that and happy that this little girl trait stayed with her throughout her life. When she opened the box that had her tennis bracelet she'd been wishing for, or when she got the news she was a grandma for the first time. She's so like a little girl when she does this. I know there's a picture of her doing this. I've got to find that picture!

Found the picture of her doing that "EEEEH" thing!

I don't even know a world without antibiotics and vaccinations. I had chicken pox as a toddler, thank you to my sister Jean, for bringing that home to me. But no measles, mumps or anything else because I was vaccinated as a child. No so my parents. When someone got the measles, or the mumps or say, scarlet fever, the entire household could be quarantined. We understand this now, those of us that didn't live during the pandemic of 1918 or these illnesses, because of Covid, but my mother understood it well her whole life. She and her sister Linda, spent time on quarantine while my mother was in kindergarten with the mumps and the measles. When Linda was little, she had scarlet fever. Scarlet fever is a bacterial infection that comes with the Strep group A bacteria. It is characterized by a high fever and a red rash, the scarlet part. Here's the kicker, antibiotics treat it, but not in the early 1940's. Doctors didn't know that antibiotics could treat all the bacterial infections we now know they can treat. So, Linda got scarlet fever, and she was quarantined. In their house, that meant she had to stay in one part of the house, and my mother and her father stayed in the other part of the house. This prevented spread and kept the whole house from being quarantined. Unfortunately, it also meant tricky planning for the family. Each day, my mom and her father would go outside, from the back of the house and knock on the window to talk to Linda, in the front of the house. They did this communicating through the glass of the window. After Linda was sleeping, they would sneak from the back of the house, outside, then back in the front door to get to the bathroom so they could bathe. This went on for several weeks. Quarantining started when the fever and rash was noticed, but didn't end until it was gone. Linda spent a lot of time on that couch, and my grandmother probably didn't leave the house that winter at all. The two cohorts were separated for a time. I guess that means there was less trouble in the Hoyt household.

My mother also had whooping cough as a child. I wonder if that plays any part in her breathing issues now? Of course, my mother smoked for years, so clearly if whooping cough had a role in her current breathing issues, it is a minor part. Before last year, it might have been funny thinking about quarantining in your house and seem like something out of tale of earlier times in human history. Now, the whole world understands the impact of quarantines. And, scarlet fever is not a laughing matter, as it used to cause widespread epidemics and death. But the thought of my mother skulking around in the dark to get a bath after her sister was asleep makes me smile a bit. Did she tiptoe? Was she scared she would lose her sister? I wonder.

Five

Golf, the Lacon Country Club, and Gay 90s

My father golfs. I don't think he did as a kid, but he did later in life, when the demands of his job diminished and his children were grown and he had more time. My Grandma Myrt and my Grandma Floye and my grandfathers were avid golfers. There is a hysterical picture of a golf event at their country club, the Lacon Country Club, of a group of women, my Grandma Myrt and Grandma Floye included, all dressed in hobo costumes of their own making. What makes this photo so funny is that both of my grandmothers are in short shorts and wearing funny hats. Generally speaking, they were usually much more fashionably, and conservatively, I might add, dressed, so seeing them like this is hilarious. I asked Linda if I could keep that picture. I want it because it is so incongruent to the people my grandmothers were.

Love this! Grandma Myrt is standing first on left, and Grandma Floye is sitting, second from right.

When my mother was growing up, I think she was dragged along to the country club so her parents could golf often and fortunately there was also a pool, or what passed for a pool in the 40's. It may have been a pond. Anyway, my mother really liked going there. Apparently, the bottom of this "pool" was very rough and my mother and her sister often came home with cut up and roughed up feet. The Augustine's, a family that lived next door to my great-grandparents, would go to the Lacon Country Club too. On several occasions, the Augustine's would return home without one of their kids, and my grandparents, along with mother, would have to take them home. This might seem strange, but there were like twenty children (not really, but there were many) in this large Italian household. Sometimes my mother would bring her friend Alice with her and they would while away the hours in the pool while my grandparents and Alice's parents golfed. Grandma Myrt golfed with several ladies, but had a tendency to get a little caustic with the younger golfers and frequently called them on the carpet for being rude on the course or violating some golden rule of country club play. She was only about 4'7" tall. Imagining her pointing her finger at a much taller young man and chastising him for committing some perceived wrong he had committed is almost comical. The people Grandma Myrt accosted probably didn't think it so funny, but I certainly do!

My mother never golfed. My aunt Cindy has picked it up later in life. To be perfectly honest, I don't see the appeal. Maybe this is because I don't really understand it, and don't see it as anything more than a way to spend a lot of time walking around in a park-like place. This will likely be another thing about me that makes me strange to my family. I wonder if my mother ever felt that way?

The day my grandmother died, as we were all standing in the hospital room, she opened her eyes, and looked around at us and said it looked nice out. It looked like a good day to golf with Chuck. She hadn't done that in a long time and she thought she'd just go golf with Chuck. She closed her eyes and that was it. She was gone. In my entire life, I only heard her talk about her husband a few times. Yet he was her last thought, and so was golf.

The Lacon Country Club is still open for business. They call themselves Timber Ridge of Lacon now, and I'm sure the golf course has been changed. Hearing all of this, and remembering Grandma Floye's last day and last words, I wish I understood golf, but I really like the fact that they played with their friends and enjoyed days at that country club.

Another thing I've learned was that my grandparents loved to dance. Back in the 1940's there was a club, called the Gay 90's where there was dancing every weekend. What this name implies is it was a throwback to times prior to the turn of the century. Remember it was in the late 1930's and 40's when this club existed. It isn't implying a throwback to 1990's. This was back when men bought women corsages, and girls wore dresses and gloves. It might have been one of the only weekend, and evening activities for young people, especially in Chillicothe IL. I know they had a Dairy Queen for a very long time, and they did get a McDonalds when I was in elementary school, but this is a small town, and when my grandmother was a young woman, it was probably even smaller. Anyway, I hear from my aunt Linda this was how my grandparents met. Mutual friends at the dance club introduced them. My grandmother was always dressed to the nines. She had this large walk-in closet and it was filled with dresses and suits, shoes and accessories. I used to play for hours in that closet when I was younger. I imagine her going out, dressed up. I wonder if they danced at home. Did her father teach my mother to dance? Did my grandparents dance in front of their children? Linda says, yes, they danced at home and their father did teach the girls to dance when they were little. I smile, as my father taught me to dance, a long time ago in our living room before my first dance in junior high school.

My mother used to really love to dance. When I was in junior high school, we had 50's dances and I got to wear my dad's letterman jacket and my mom made me a poodle skirt. Mom and Dad taught me to jitter-bug. Whenever there was a wedding or an event where there was dancing, my parents were always out there. I think she must have gotten her love of dancing from her parents. My parents' song is I Can't Help Falling in Love by Elvis. Whenever I hear that song, I see my parents dancing. I love to watch them dance. They seemed to float across the floor in the waltz. I never could figure out how to waltz, it might have something to do with my controlling nature. The waltz seems to require a passive participant, and I have trouble with that, but my parents look like they were born dancing together. It's probably because they have been together so long, but watching them always made me smile.

My mother doesn't like to dance much anymore though. I think it makes her afraid she'll fall. Dad sometimes teases her as he helps her out of her chair and she holds onto his hand longer than is needed. He says, oh, you want to dance? And then he tries to get her to dance in their living room. She starts her No, no, no, no, no. He lets her go before she gets scared or falls. I miss watching them dance.

Clearly there is this legacy as well, the dancing and golfing. My family has so many stories. Thinking of all of these little moments I am again very angry about Alzheimer's. It's taking so much from my mother. I'm starting to understand just how much.

Six

～

Alice, Gene McKay, and the Augustine's

There are a few people that play a big part in my mother's childhood. One of these is Alice Metcalf, formerly Alice Lee. She was a good friend of my mother's from before they started school, when they were three years old. Alice and her family moved to Chillicothe and lived in the upstairs apartment in Grandma Elsie and Grandpa Lee's house on Cedar Street. Alice and my mother met when my mother was at her grandparent's visiting, and they became fast friends. By the way, her name wasn't Alice Metcalf then, but that is how I know her. When I was younger, visiting her house, we called her Aunt Alice. That's the kind of friend she was to my mom.

Alice was another of my mother's cohorts. The good news is that my mother spread her antics around, the bad news, she seemed to have many followers! Alice and my mother played together often. On one such play day, when they were around five or six, they decided to perhaps get even with a neighbor that was protective of their garden of beautiful flowers. Alice and my mother trampled the garden and probably caused quite a stir! My mother often spoke of Alice and their birthday parties, walks to the candy store and their fun in high school. My aunt Linda shared with me once that she and Alice didn't hit it off so well, or at least had one day where they didn't like each other. Apparently, Aunt Alice played overzealously with Linda's doll and broke it. Linda, fresh off the stop swearing game, and young, started referring to Alice as "that damn Adice Lee". Again, I'm reminded of the strong women in my family. Funny, but strong!

Alice remained a friend to my mother throughout their lives. Later, when my mother moved into the married units after marrying my father while he was still a student at Western Illinois University, Alice assisted with her move. She visited often and visited with my mother when she resided in that same apartment Alice and her family first lived in just prior to my father's last year in college. During these visits, they would play card games and laugh and laugh. When I was younger, we would stop in and visit Aunt Alice when we went to Chillicothe. She has been a fixture at important events, like when my father was inducted into hall of fames at his high school. Interestingly, Jan recently gave my mother a doll to focus her Alzheimer's need to hold on to something and the doll gave her an object that was appropriate for her to hold. Mom named the doll Alice. Clearly, this is indicative of that long-standing friendship. If I showed my mother a picture of Alice, she might not recognize her, but she understood down deep that Alice was a friend.

Mom and cousin Gene playing in the
washtub

Another playmate of my mother's and one that she remained close with his entire life is her cousin, Gene McKay. Mom and Gene played together, sat in washtubs of water together, and vacationed together with their grandparents. Gene McKay's mother was Helen Hoyt, my grandfather's sister. Aunt Helen liked to knit, crochet and sew. We have several sets of baby clothing she made that have been passed along all the females of our family. They're all with my granddaughter now, the youngest strong female in our family. Anyway, Gene was a constant companion to both my mother and aunt Linda. Gene's parents bought that house that Grandma Elsie lived in, the one with the upstairs apartment that Alice and her family lived in, at some point. That house, in fact, plays a pivotal role in my family's lives. My parents lived in that upstairs apartment the summer before my older sister was born, just before my father graduated from college. My aunt Linda and her husband lived there when they were newlyweds, until their daughter was almost two years old, and my aunt Cindy and her husband also lived there when they were newlyweds. It was the place to start out for most of my family. I visited this apartment when Cindy and her husband lived there. Last time I was in Chillicothe, I drove by it. As all things do when viewed with an adult eye, it looked smaller than I remembered as a child. It looks a little worn and shabby about the edges, much like the faded photographs of my family near that house now look.

I wonder what it was like, moving back into that house for my mother, after it had been her grandmother's home, Alice's home, and cousin Gene's home. So much of her life was spent there. I'm sure it changed as each family moved in and out, but what memories!

While my parents were residing in that tiny little apartment at Western Illinois University, Gene and Aunt Linda visited often. One of those visits, my mom and Linda decided to splurge on steaks. It was early in the 1960s and most people, including my parents, lived on very little income. It seems strange to contemplate bread costing ten cents, but remember, incomes were probably more like a few thousand dollars a year. Of course, everything cost less, but it was a big deal to buy steaks and they were probably expensive by 1960's standards. Unfortunately, in this tiny three-room apartment, the kitchen was tucked into the corner, right next to the bathroom. Opening the oven and the refrigerator at the same time was probably impossible. While Gene, my mother and Linda were gathered, or squeezing into the kitchen, my mother went to check on those expensive steaks and pulled open the oven door and the steaks came sliding out the oven and went right across the kitchen floor. They landed perfectly, just in front of the toilet! After they all had a good laugh, that probably included someone falling on the floor, the steaks were retrieved, rinsed off in the sink and put back in the oven.

After my grandfather died suddenly, Pappy, who adored his daughter Floye, decided that he would add onto the back of his house and create a place for Floye and her three girls to come and live. This would allow him to help care for all of them and support his daughter. His practice was in the office in the front, he and Grandma Myrt lived in the space next to the office, and Grandma Floye and her girls lived in the back. Unfortunately, no one realized that this was to be short-lived as Pappy died soon after they moved in. That left the front of house for my Grandma Myrt, and the back of the house for my Grandma Floye, my mother and two aunts. They shared a kitchen. It must have been interesting, five women living closely together. I want to convey that I mean that very facetiously, and I can't imagine anything worse than five women residing together in one house, sharing one kitchen, two bathrooms and very little closet space!

Living next door to this collection of women were the Augustine's. A quintessential Italian family, they had nine children, I think. Some were the same age as my mother and aunt Linda but most of them were older. Things were crazy at the Augustine house with all those kids, and naturally all conversations were more likely loud Italian arguments. Often, the Augustine children would run over and ask to use the bathroom at my mother's house. The reason for this? They were only allowed to flush their toilet so many times in a day and inevitably one of those Augustine children had to go after the last flush of the day. I don't know if this limitation was a plumbing issue, or a family rule or to keep the water bill low, but it cracks me up, that a big house full of kids, would be running next door to use the one bathroom that my grandmother shared with her three daughters when they had a living room, bedroom and bathroom, basically.

Naturally because of the many children, and chaos in their house, what my mother and aunts remember about the Augustine's is the food found under and on their couch and between the cushion and the base of their couch. Yuk! I'm sure, with the quiet all-girls situation at their house, the rancorous laughing and fun at the neighbors seemed strange, but since I'm married to an Italian, I know and can tell you, don't cross that Italian momma. She'll chase you down with a wooden spoon! Aunt Linda tells me that momma Augustine was not like that, and that they were always offered some of the food that was perpetually on the stove in the Augustine kitchen.

What do I remember about the Augustine's? Well, first, one of their boys was drafted during the Viet Nam war and rather than respond to the draft, he moved to Canada. I remember hearing Grandma Floye talking about it. She didn't agree with what he did, based on the comments I heard her make. At some point, momma Augustine became grandma Augustine, and I played with a granddaughter in my grandma's backyard. Today, I can't remember her name, but we had fun, that I remember. Grandma Augustine had a large garden in her backyard when I was growing up and as I remember we were told we couldn't go near it. An admonishment I clearly understood and obeyed. We were not to mess with her plants. She had huge sunflowers bordering her garden that I was always fascinated with. That granddaughter and I, or perhaps it was my cousin Janet and I, once had a big fight with the neighbor boy that lived behind my grandmother. I remember that too. His last name was McGann. I referred to them as "MeeGans". I got in trouble for hitting that boy. I remember it seemed unfair. I'm pretty sure that boy started it, by insulting or threatening my little cousin or friend. You never know though, I was a bit of tomboy when I was kid, and probably would have been ready to tussle right along with the boys. It's funny how your memories play back like old home movies when you think back to your childhood.

As I drove by this place, where my mother spent her teenage years, and where I remember my grandmother teaching me to paint, I think about all these people that meant so much to my mother. How rich her life was for knowing them. The friendships, the laughter, the impact they had on her life. Of course, now my grandmother's house is gone. So is the Augustine's house. There's a car wash there now. It makes me sad. The loss of that place that was so important to my mom, and me. I pulled in the alley that ran behind my grandmother's house the last time I was in Chillicothe. I sat, where I figured their driveway was, and the old garage. I didn't see the car wash; I saw the big white house with the stairwell leading to the door. The grassy patio area where Grandma had her metal chairs sitting, waiting for a lazy afternoon of reading. I wondered what it looked like when my mother moved in there. How she must have felt a little lost without her father, a bit shaken by the change, right before she started high school. Was she excited about this change? Comforted by her grandfather? I wish I could ask her. I have no way to understand what that would be like. I still have my father. He was always there for me and my siblings. He's devoted to my mother and to his children. I can't even imagine not having him in my life. What must that be like? I shudder at the thought. And again, at all my mother is losing with this disease.

Seven

⌒∾

Band, Cheerleading, and the Siblings in the Cave

Mom playing her
trombone on her
front sidewalk

I know this is going to make my mother sound a bit like a geek, at least by the standards I grew up with, but she played the trombone. You know, the instrument that has the long brass loop like piece that you push out and pull in? She's also only about five feet, three inches tall. But here's the thing, she was really good at it, and I think she played it because her grandfather played the same instrument. Anyway, she was so good, that when she was in eighth grade, she was invited to play with the high school band. And remember, she was taking lessons from when she was much younger each Saturday. That seems like a really big deal, and it probably was, but keep in mind, my parent's high school graduating class had like ninety kids in it. There might just been no decent trombone players that year. Of course, if you look at the yearbooks, the band is really big given the size of the classes. So maybe it was not a geeky thing to do, but a cool thing to do back then.

All kidding aside, she was good. She won all kinds of awards, and was first chair. It's hard to imagine that being cool, but in 1958 it was, because at the same time she was playing in the band, my mother, yes, my mother, was named most popular girl of her senior class! Imagine that?! I think back to my high school days and those voted most popular in my class. They knew almost everyone in our class, they were friends with many and did all kinds of things. Was that what my mother was like in high school? If you look at her high school yearbooks, it sure seems like she was involved with a lot of things. She is in just about every club there was, in the band, attending dances. She was busy!

Anyway, she kept that trombone for a really long time. It was in our attic when I was growing up. When we'd go up there for something, I'd always ask her to play it. She did once. Oh, and Aunt Linda played in the band too. She won awards as well. So did Alice. I played the violin for a few years. It just wasn't in keeping with my tomboy lifestyle so I gave it up. Also, as a left-handed person growing up in the 1970s, everything was taught from the perspective of the right-handed world. That meant sometimes you were simply told at the end of the instructions to do the opposite if you were a lefty. My kids both played in the band. They were very musically inclined. I suspect they got that from my mother. She used to insist on coming with me to watch my kids play, and my kids absolutely loved looking up and seeing their grandparents in the stands for all of their events. This is what ties our family together. In fact, one summer, after football practice, my son and his friends were out on the deck, eating everything I laid out for them, when one of those boys asked about my son's fan club. Apparently, my children basked in the understanding from their friends that they had the biggest fan club at all events. I looked out as I heard this conversation and my son smiled. He said he never heard anyone up in the stands, but he always knew his grandparents and parents were there. In that moment, I'm brought back to my childhood when my extended family would travel a couple of hours for graduations, birthdays and important games. I wish my mother remembered this. I wish she felt the warmth of love from her grandchildren for the biggest fan club. I hope my children told her how much her support meant to them while she still understood what they meant.

In addition to being first chair in the band, my mother was also a cheerleader. Those two things seem a bit incongruent, but it's true. I've seen pictures. Now, back in the 1950s, cheerleaders were not gymnasts like they are today. There weren't cheerleading contests where girls were being thrown through the air. When my mother was in high school, the girls simply clapped, cheered and supported the sports teams. Here's the cool part, my father played football, basketball and baseball in high school. Isn't it cute, the cheerleader and the co-captain? Yes, it's a little cliché and kind of corny, but I like this little tidbit about my parents. She in her long cheerleading skirt and he in his football uniform, walking home. While my mother was winning band contests, my father was making all conference teams, participating in undefeated football seasons, and making plays on the field and court. As I look through their yearbook, I understand some things better. Now I know why they pushed us the way they did when we were growing up, my siblings and I. If you're going to do something, do it well, that's what my father said once. My parent's drive was passed on, as my siblings and I are all just as driven. It's kind of our legacy, I think.

Part of their drive meant my parents were also in all kinds of clubs when they were in high school. The future homemakers of America, the yearbook staff, student government, Spanish club, which my father was president his senior year, chorus and the C Club. They were busy! I'm not entirely certain what the C Club did, but there is a picture in the yearbook. It's actually one of the only times my parents are pictured together in all their doings outside of dance pictures. And can you believe they had a future homemakers of America club? What did they meet about? How to get stains out of fabric? Seriously this seems very strange to me, even a decade or so after my mother participated in this kind of a club. I'm sure it was what was later referred to as Home Economics, but I find it all funny. By the time I was in high school, girls were not thinking about homemaking, we were thinking about careers and college. All of this is a little hard to contemplate by today's standards. Kids today tend to be focused by high school and devoted to only one or two activities. Not so in 1958. I wonder if they were ever home. With all those clubs, and sports and band and cheerleading, when did they study?

While all these clubs and band and sports were going on, there was also some pranks, dares and fun happening. Linda usually tagged along with my mother and her friends on their weekend activities. This sometimes included bowling, and sometimes, when there wasn't a dance or band competition or anything else going on, this group of girls found other ways to amuse themselves. One such weekend night, the girls decided to go out of town and see if they could find and maybe startle the siblings that lived outside of town in a cave. Yes, I said a cave. It wasn't really a rock cave, but more like a self-constructed mound of rock and dirt and grass in the middle of an abandoned pasture. In the late 1940s and early 1950s, self-sufficiency was still an option for people. If you could farm, and maintain livestock you didn't need to have a job. Sounds strange, right? These siblings were Mandy and Henry. I don't know their last names or what became of them. They occasionally came into town. To see the doctor, Pappy, my great-grandfather, and to get some supplies. I'm sure there was quite a bit of mystique about these two in town, even in 1950. So, the girls, including Linda, a few other friends, a friend Marge, with a leg in a cast, set out west of town looking for this cave. Before you wonder, I do not know the reason for Marge being in that cast, it wasn't part of the story, but they did manage to get Marge over a barbed-wire fence unharmed. I don't think they got as far as any caves, and much to my dismay, I don't know if they were caught, chased off, or just gave up. For some reason, after all the stories being told, this one didn't get its ending right away. I found out, after checking back with Linda that they gave up out of fear of not being able to get Marge back safely. That ending feels like the balloon deflating, but that's the story I was told. I'm a little suspect, however. I would have loved to be there, watching these girls sneak across fields and climb over fences. Since I know that my mother rarely wore pants, I wonder how they managed this in skirts? Maybe when I retell this story, I should give it a better ending?

It's strange that I never heard this from my mother. We all have one of these adventures in our past, don't we? The story we don't tell anyone even years after it happened? And those we never tell our children? You know, you parents, the ones that might make you look hypocritical given your rules for your children? I have one of these. Yes, I'm telling one of mine here. When I was a pre-teen, likely 11 or 12, several friends of mine and I went to the back grassy area behind the elementary school. We liked to trample down some of that grass in a circle and sit out there. It felt like we were hiding from everyone, even though if we stood up, we could see the school, the church, and some of our houses. Anyway, one of those times we were back there, a fire was started. You guessed it; the whole field went up in flames. What were we thinking? Lighting a fire in a dried, grassy field, right? We of course scattered. The fire department showed up, put the fire out and probably searched for the culprits that started it. I don't ever remember them combing the neighborhood, nor do I ever remember being asked about it. I was there. I was not the fire starter, but I was there. I never told my mother. Maybe that's why she didn't tell me about her cave adventure.

Mom and I have a lot in common, I've come to learn. She was a bit of a troublemaker, a talented musician, a cheerleader, a friend, and a girl trying to have fun. I was a bit of troublemaker, a talented artist, not a cheerleader, a friend, and a girl that was trying to have fun.

Eight

ᴗᴥᴗ

Love, Love, and More Love

No understanding of my mother is complete without a story of my parents meeting, dating and marrying. Really, what I'm talking about is when they fell in love. In an age where almost half of all marriages end in divorce, my parents are a bit of an anomaly. They just celebrated their 61st wedding anniversary. I think that's amazing. But, in my family, not really. Linda and her husband, Cindy and her husband, and virtually all of my grandparents were and are still together their whole lives. Not simply astounding, this is the most profound part of my family's legacy.

I believe the legacy of love and devotion between the couples of my family began with Grandma Myrt and Pappy. Although scandalous, they must have loved deeply to take the chances they took to be together. I know there was love between my grandma Floye and her husband. How do I know this? Because of the tales of them dancing, and golfing and laughing. Because of the pictures I have held in my hands of them together. Together was the word that I think of when I think of them. Also, I know that my grandmother grieved for him for a very long time, probably her whole life. I don't remember there being a picture of him anywhere in her house when I was a child. I asked her about him frequently, but only once did she entertain my questions. In the summer when I was growing up, I would spend a week or two with grandma. We would paint, read and go shopping. I would walk up to Jane's, the dress shop she worked at, and we would go to the pool hall for lunch. One evening during such a visit, I asked her about my grandfather. She looked up from her crossword puzzle and held my gaze for a minute and then looked out the window. She answered a few of my questions. At some point, she muttered that she'd had enough and I knew better and stopped the questioning.

Aunt Linda told me once that only one time, long after my mother had married, and after Linda had married, my grandmother asked Aunt Cindy one night if she would mind it if her mother went on a date. She had apparently been asked out and Cindy said she didn't mind. Later, Linda said, Grandma said she just didn't like it. She never saw that man again, as far as I know. Then, her last thoughts and last words were about her husband. It was the first and only time I ever heard her call him by name. That is profound love to me. It is also very sad. She spent so much of her life without him.

My parents met in high school, during their freshman year. One of the funniest parts of their story is that my mother asked my father out on their first date. Ok, it was the Sadie Hawkins dance. That is the spring dance where the girls ask the boys. We called it turnabout when I was in high school. At some point, when I was interrogating my mother about her relationship with my father, my mother describes a girl at her school who also wanted to ask my father to this dance. My father had taken this girl to the homecoming dance earlier in that school year, but my mother wanted to ask him to Sadie Hawkins. As my mother tells it, she got there first, purposefully. This adds to the story as far as I'm concerned because it makes my mother look like she was pursuing my father. I also like that she was assertive enough to make this move. Aside from the homecoming dance, earlier that school year, which my mother attended with Jim Arnold, my father is the only person my mother ever dated. My father shares that history as he went to homecoming with someone else, but then never dated another girl.

This little dance was the beginning of their lives together. They dated all through high school. They went to all the dances together, double-dating with Linda and her date once she got to high school, I'm sure. They had picnics at Shore Acres, and probably went to parties with their friends. I already know from the yearbook, they participated in many clubs together, and her being a cheerleader, and his being an athlete, they must have spent many Friday nights and weekend days at sporting events. After high school, my mother went to Bloomington, IL to the nursing school at St. Joseph hospital, and my father went to Western Illinois University in Macomb, IL. During their third year, they decided they could wait no longer and planned to elope. However, the rules back in 1961 were vastly different than they are today. Back then, a girl could marry without parental approval after she was eighteen years old. Boys couldn't until they were twenty-one. My parents married in January of the year they would have turned 21, but not until later that year. Because of this, my grandfather also attended the elopement so he could provide consent. There are no pictures of their wedding day, no cake was served, no flowers and no dancing. At the end of that weekend, they both returned to their respective schools. My mother was only a few months from graduating, as the nursing program was not a full four-year program, but three continuous years of training. The nursing program was, however, run by nuns. In 1961 that meant only single ladies were accepted into the program. As luck would have it, one my mother's friends, while very excited about the news of the nuptials, sent my mother a lovely card addressed to Mrs. Jerry Blew. My mother was discovered, and sent packing by the nuns a few short weeks before graduation. This is when my mother moved into the married units with my father at Western.

What surprises me about this story is the stability of my parents' relationship. When I asked my mother if they ever argued or had troubles when they were in high school or college, she laughed me off. Aunt Linda, however, does recall at least one day my father spent with them when my mother and father barely spoke, sitting at opposite ends of the couch and there is even a photo taken on this day, when my mother and father do not look so happy. What also surprises me is that my parents have really never dated anyone else. In all their lives, they've only been with one another. When I marveled at this probably when I was in high school, it was pointed out by my mother that she did attend homecoming that fall of her freshman year with another boy, but that was the only other date she was on. My parents have been together more than 65 years. That's incredible. What's most incredible about their story is that they seem more in love now than they did when I was younger. True, children have a funny way of viewing their parents' relationship and it likely isn't until later as they grow older that children get a truer sense of the love between their parents, but I've witnessed this relationship over my entire life, and they are more loving and more cocooned by that love now than they have ever been. I have many memories of my parents laughing with friends, teasing each other, kissing and dancing.

One of my favorites!

It's daunting actually, when you look at the marriages in my family. There are my parents, of course, but there is also that profound love between my grandmother and her husband, and my great grandmother and my great grandfather. It doesn't stop there.

Aunt Linda knew my uncle Larry all through high school, although he dated someone else most of those years. Sometime after high school, Linda was with cousin Gene at Blarney's Castle, the local pizza joint, when Larry noticed her on a crisp September or October night. He thought she was on a date, but once that little bit of confusion was cleared up, they began dating. They were married that Christmas Eve. Yes, I am talking a few short months later. Clearly, they were certain they had found the right person to spend their lives with. Aunt Cindy met my uncle Stu on a blind date set up by Stu's cousin, Cathy, who taught English at the Chillicothe high school. Stu was one of a set of twin brothers of a farmer. He was drafted during Viet Nam, and spent the entire rest of his career at Caterpillar. That blind date started their path to the alter. They were married on a very hot summer day when I was seven years old. I remember the bright yellow dresses we wore. I, along with Jean and my mother and aunt were among Cindy's bridesmaids. At some events later in our family, like when Jean got married, and when we had bridal showers, Linda would pull out that yellow dress, that she could still wear, and share that with us. It serves as the opening of many family stories and a lot of laughter. While there is a lovely picture of Linda and Larry cutting a wedding cake in Grandma Myrt's dining room, and an album full of pictures of Cindy's wedding, there are no picture of my parents' wedding day. That may be a good thing, however, because we make fun of those lemon-yellow dresses any, and every single, time we're all together!

At the end of the day, this is my family's greatest legacy. Those five women, living together in that house, sharing a kitchen. They left the most powerful legacy to their children. Devotion and love. These marriages represent the best of some of the best people I know. Further, these are the some of the greatest love stories as far as I'm concerned. When you think of the great love stories, you think *Love Story*, with Ali McGraw and Ryan O'Neal and *Pride and Prejudice*, with Lizzy and Mr. Darcy. For me, up with these stories are the stories of my parents, my aunts and uncles, and my grandparents.

This is why it was so hard to tell my parents when I made the decision to divorce my first husband. It made me feel like such a failure, a failure to this legacy. Naturally, my family and my parents rallied around me during that difficult time and didn't judge me. When Rich prepared to propose to me, he asked permission from our three children, not my father. When I explained this to my father, he simply smiled, said nothing, but we both understood, I had found the right one to spend my life with. Rich is also very much like my father. What is it that they say? Every girl marries her father. I guess I had to get much closer to that to find the right one. Now I feel like I'm living up to this loving legacy. Even so, every day I judge myself against these people who are so devoted to one another and their families.

Now that my parents are facing Alzheimer's, their relationship has changed. My father is sometimes as much a parent to my mother as he is husband. When the disease started to take hold, my mother would bicker with my father. She would complain and push back on taking medicine, taking a shower, getting dressed, pretty much everything. Explaining to my mother for the hundredth day in a row that pills needed to be swallowed, not chewed occasionally frustrated the daylights out of my father. He would get angry with her and walk away. Sometimes he would get angry with us for doing too much for her. At times witnessing this anger between my parents and their bickering makes me sad. The fact that I so rarely saw them argue throughout my life, and now this terrible disease was causing strive bothered me greatly. How dare this disease take away this away from my parents! He's focused his life on her care, and she pushes back and isn't always nice to him. I know this is part of the disease, but I hate seeing them act in a way that is not reflective of the love they have for each other. Just another reason to hate this disease. But then, I will be riding in the car with them and watch my mother reach out to my father to hold his hand. Even in the depths of this disease, she knows she can reach for him. It calms her, and in those moments, I understand the enormity of their love for one another. My father will sometimes walk by my mother sitting in her chair and lean over her and give her a kiss. She will smile at him, sometimes, and reach up and pull on his shirt to bring him back down to her and he will laugh and ask her if she wants another one. It's in these moments that I find some comfort, and see clearly the love they have had for one another their whole lives, it seems.

Nine

～

Shore Acres, Your Best Behavior, the Flyswatter, and the Yearbook

Chillicothe, as far as I know, is known for only a few things. One, the railroad went through there first. Then there was a quarry where stone was extracted for years. It sits on the Illinois River. But what I knew it most for when I was younger was Shore Acres. Shore Acres is a park that sits on the river, at one point had a golf course, but what I know it for is the pool. It was the park that contained the public pool. It's where I learned to swim as a child.

When my parents were growing up, the pool was smaller, and located near the mansion that resided on the property. During that time, the Taylor's lived there. Mom and Dad went to school with Ron and Tim Taylor. Mr. Taylor was the coach of the football and baseball teams at their high school.

My father worked at Shore Acres. My father had a lot of interesting jobs when he was younger. During the time my sister was born, he delivered milk. During high school he did all kinds of jobs at Shore Acres. He painted that mansion. He tells us a story of this painting project where he was put out an attic window, with a rope tied around his stomach to try to reach the peak of that mansion to paint. He also said it took nearly three years to complete that painting job. I remember going to this mansion to see Mrs. Taylor when I was young. The pool that had been there when my parents were young, was still there, but it was filled with water, leaves and gunk.

Mom, surprisingly in pants

My parents spent time at the park there, had picnics there with their friends. Later, I went to ball games of my cousins there, and spent many summer days at the new public pool. When I was about ten or so years old, the Illinois River flooded really badly. We took a drive down by the park when we were in town and saw that the water had risen well into the park, flooded that old pool completely and pulled a house off the foundation that was floating by the old mansion. I remember standing on the back seat of our car, looking out the back window thinking about all the things a family had lost in that house floating down the river. Sometimes that's how I feel about Alzheimer's. That sad moment watching someone's life float down the river, is just like watching my mother lose all of her memories.

My mother grew up in town. Her grandfather was the town doctor. In the 1940's and 50's, this must have seemed like the epitome of high class. By today's standards, probably not so much, but then, to the two siblings living in a cave, and to those living out of town, these town people must have seemed wealthy in a lot of ways. My father grew up out of town. His parents moved to Chillicothe when my father was an infant. My paternal grandparents lived in Missouri before they moved to

Chillicothe. They were from different religious groups. In fact, those two groups rarely intermingled. Their marriage meant they had to leave both of their religions. After engaging in a myriad of jobs, from nursing, to farming, to factory work, they moved when my grandfather was employed by the railroad. When my father was nearing high school, my grandfather was in a terrible accident at the railyard. He was basically run over by a slow-moving train at conductor shift change. After being in traction for months with a broken back, and a settlement with the railroad, my father's family made some changes to their home. They added on, and for the first time, enjoyed indoor plumbing. Regardless of this, my father, his sister and brother were always provided for. My grandmother would cook my father a large T-bone steak each Friday before football games. However, I have learned that my grandmother saw my mother's family as more privileged in some way, probably because they lived in town. Later, when my mother and father were dating, my father would spend weekend days at my mother's house. Sometimes he would bring his younger sister, Janet, along with him. The first time this occurred, my father's mother told Janet she had to wear a nice dress and be on her best behavior when she went to the doctor's house.

When I reflect on this, a few thoughts come instantly. I know my Grandma Myrt was a bit of tyrant about who sat in her living room, and both my Grandma Floye and Grandma Myrt, though small in stature, would not take any crap from anyone, but my aunt Janet is tall. In fact, my father's family is a great deal taller than my mother's family. I can't imagine a situation where Janet might be intimidated by two small, grey-haired women. However, as I reflect on this little bit of a story longer, I do admit that in both my mother's and my father's families, it was a set-in stone rule that you respected people that were older than you. Perhaps Janet appeared timid to my grandmothers by virtue of this long-standing rule. Then, I wonder if my father's mother knew about Grandma Myrt's swearing problem? Would that have changed the directions Janet was given? I wonder. And, recently I learned that although my mother always thought she was seen as some sort of invading force for taking her first-born son away, in fact, my paternal grandmother was always a bit in awe of my mother. This made her more quiet, and unsure and likely was the cause of my mother's distance. It's a shame neither of them bothered to talk about this when they had a chance. My mother might have known that my grandmother saw her as an expert in almost everything and often feared she had the wrong shoes on or something.

As I stated earlier, the members of my family have what I like to refer to as our signature story. That one event of our lives that we can never be allowed to live down. The one that to all other members of the family seem to signify the nature of our personalities. For my mother, that story is the flyswatter story.

It is important for the retelling of this story to anyone outside the family to set the stage. My mother was in high school, likely a senior. She lived in that white house, with the second story entrance on top of a long cement stairwell outside of their living room. At the bottom of that stairwell was a little garden area that for as long as I can remember contained several metal chairs and tables. There was a clothes line in the backyard, a swing set, a three-foot-high cinderblock enclosed fire area to burn garbage and a ramshackle old garage facing the alley. The importance of these details will soon become clear. One bright afternoon, my mother decided she knew better than her mother and talked back when she was told to do something. My grandmother said what probably every mother says the first time a child talks back, "What did you say?" My mother's response was to repeat what she said. My grandmother rose from her chair, likely to deliver the slapping my mother probably deserved and my mother made the choice that all children make at least once in their lives when they know they are about to be spanked. She ran. My grandmother told her to come back or she would get it worse, and my mother ran out the door and down those stairs into the backyard. My grandmother, who generally I remember as one cool customer, picked up the metal-handled flyswatter and went after my mother out the door. After a lap around the fire area, and at least some dodging of the clothesline pole, my grandmother caught my mother and gave her several whacks with that flyswatter on the back of her legs.

Flyswatters today are totally made of plastic and can barely kill flies.

In 1957 they were made of metal and the metal was twisted together to form a handle and to hold the square of netting used to kill the flies. Those twists resulted in edges of metal. My mother told us this story when we were kids, and of course, I've heard it many times from my grandmother, especially when she was trying to impart some instruction she wanted to be sure we listened to. With each telling, the wounds from this flyswatter seem to get worse. Also, what my mother said sometimes gets more or less disrespectful, depending on the storyteller. Anyone and, in fact, everyone who ever hears this story, is usually by this point, doubled over with laughter. The idea of a teenager being chased around the small yard full of obstacles with a flyswatter wielding petite grey-haired lady is a comedy, for sure. When we were young, this tale was brought out whenever one of us even looked like we were going to disobey our mother. She would threaten us with the flyswatter. If Grandma Floye did it, surely our mother would do it too, right? I'm sure it had the exact affect they were after. As we got older, it started to move much closer in likeness to an old road runner cartoon. As I have learned more about my mother, I recognize its signature status for the truth. My mother, like her mother and grandmother before her, was a sassy smart-mouth!

I hope, I mean, I really hope, my mother remembers this story. If she forgets everything else about her childhood, the legacies of the amazing women of her family, even if she forgets the great love story of her and my father, I hope she remembers this story. I hope Alzheimer's doesn't take this from her. It is quintessentially her.

One thing my mother and I share is that we both worked on our high school yearbooks. In fact, we both were editors of our high school yearbooks. In my case, I was the only editor in chief of both my junior and senior year yearbooks. My mother was co-editor in chief of her senior yearbook. The other co-editor in chief was Dana Stiers. One of the tasks of the editor in chief, or in this case, co-editors in chief is to write something for the yearbook. A conclusion to the year, the effort to put the yearbook together and to thank the people that helped to make the yearbook a completed project. When you have one editor in chief, he or she writes this alone. When you have co-editors in chief, there should be two such end-of-year notes included in the yearbook. Not so in my mother's senior yearbook. Dana decided that she wanted to do this end of year note, and she alone wanted the glory of having her name attached to this time-honored tradition of closing out the yearbook. I may be taking liberties by declaring her thoughts and feelings, and you might say I am misjudging the situation, but I would say no to that. I don't like the idea of anyone hurting my mother in any way and I think that's what happened here. And, I think this stinks.

Why, you might be asking now, do I feel I have to include this. Why does it matter 63 years later whose name is on that last page of the yearbook? For starters, it makes me mad that someone hurt my mother. She harbored some resentment for some time about this as I heard about it and saw the hurt in my mother's face many times over the years. But the bigger issue for me is that selfishness is timeless. It was a pretty selfish thing to do, and they were supposed to be friends.

I met Dana some years ago, she now lives near my parents in Florida as her husband is retired from the US Air Force. She organized a trip to a theater production of Cats one spring when I was in town visiting my parents. She acted like she and mother were best friends. It was then that it started to matter to me. I know it is totally my issue, but I can't stand it when people act as though you are friends when you barely know one another. I also do not like people that are so focused on their own desire for notoriety or advancement they disregard the cost to those around them. In Dana's end of year note, she thanked nearly every member of the yearbook staff, except my mother. This is one memory I'm not concerned about my mother losing to Alzheimer's.

Ten

~

Nurses' Training, Elopement, Being Exposed, and Running Out of Money

Nurse Lee

Of all the mysteries that make up my mother, one that stands out is what made her want to become a nurse. No one I spoke to that knew her as a young girl remembers the moment when she first said I want to be a nurse. Perhaps it was the sudden death of her father, and then soon after her grandfather? Maybe it was always in her nature to care for others. I don't really know. Maybe I'll ask her and she'll have one of those moments of total clarity that seem to come less and less frequently and she'll give me the answer I've been seeking, or, more likely, this will be one of those little facts that remains a mystery.

In 1958 when my mother and father graduated from high school, they had, at least in writing, committed their love to one another. I know because they both retain their yearbooks and there is a similar note from each of them to the other in the pages of their yearbook. Reason won out over young love and they decided to follow their individual dreams. I'm sure they felt that the few years of college would not deter their love for one another and so my mother left for Bloomington and my father left for Macomb to embark on their college careers.

The nurses' training my mother attended was run by nuns through St. Joseph Hospital in Bloomington, IL. She stayed in a dormitory with other girls. The program was only offered to young single women. No men welcome, no older women seeking a new career welcome. Remember it was both 1958 and it was a program attached to a Catholic chartered hospital. So, Mom moved into the dormitory, met other girls and began attending classes. It is there that she learned to make beds in a tight hospital format. We refer to this in our family as hospital corners. You know, when the ends of the sheets are tucked in so tight and in such a way that they will never come out from under the mattress? That's how my mother learned to make beds, and that is how she taught her children to make beds. It drives my husband nuts! So, naturally I do it to our bed all the time.

When I asked my mother as a child what she learned in nurses' training she talked about giving shots, cleaning and administering medications. There are some pictures of my mother in her uniform. She reminds me of Mary Poppins or some such movie character with the white dress, cap and cape. Once she talked about dissecting. I won't go into those details here. You're welcome. I'm sure that particular subject came up because of questions from my younger brother, Jerry. Anyway, the nurses' program ran continuously for three years, so in theory, my mother was going to graduate almost one full year before my father. I'm sure they talked about that as they prepared to leave for school. I'm sure it also came up when they saw each other over Christmas and other holiday breaks. I know it came up sometime before January of 1961 because that is when my parents eloped.

Little Hawaiian party at nurses' training

My mother was set to be done with nurses' training that spring. I'm sure they thought it was a perfect plan to go ahead and make it official before they each returned to school that winter. I mean, they only had a few months for mother to graduate and then she was probably headed to Macomb anyway. So, a plan was hatched. I don't mean they did this in total secrecy. They couldn't. First of all, the laws dictated at that time that my father could not marry without parental consent. He was not yet twenty-one years old. Some parent needed to be told to provide this consent. As such, I'm sure that my father told his parents and my mother told her mother about their plans. Again, it was 1961 so there were still such things as justice of the peace, where young eager couples could go to get married. On January 7, 1961, my parents married, and at the end of that weekend, he went back to Macomb and she went back to Bloomington.

> Hoyt-Blew
> Marriage Is
> Announced
> Mrs. Charles Hoyt of 516 N. Fourth st. announces the recent marriage of her daughter, Lee Elizabeth to Jerry Lee Roy Blew, son of Mr. and Mrs. Homer Blew of R.R. 1, Chillicothe.
> Mrs. Blew is a senior at St. Joseph's School of Nursing in Bloomington. Mr. Blew is a junior at Western Illinois University in Macomb.

All of this would have been fine if my mother hadn't received a lovely cad from a friend addressed Mrs. Jerry Blew. She was summoned to the nun's office and told she must leave the program despite the fact that she had only weeks to graduate. She'd broken the rule and was married. Mom's friend Alice came and helped with my mother's hasty move to the married units at Western Illinois University. And, despite not graduating fully from the program, my mother began working at the local hospital, you guessed it, as a nurse. After they left Macomb, I am not aware of my mother having another job as a nurse. She began having children and focused her caregiving on that effort. She never returned to nursing. I often wonder if the desire to nurse was tied up with her desire to care for others and the needs of her four children filled that need to care in her. Having changed careers at least twice during my adult life, I know that your ambitions and needs do change. I guess it's possible she just decided she wanted to do something else. I doubt I will ever know because I bring this up with her with some frequency now. She sometimes can't grasp that she needs to swallow pills now. Thank you, Alzheimer's. When she tries to chew pills, I try to talk to her as if she totally understands, having been through nurses' training and teaching me so many things about first aide, health and medicines, and she just keeps chewing. It can be very frustrating, trying to reason with an Alzheimer's patient. It's like trying to herd cats.

Back to the nurses' training. At some point, in that winter just after my parents got married, but before she was dismissed from the program, my mother was home for the weekend or a holiday and she was spending the evening at the bowling alley with her sister, Lollie and some friends. I'm sure they were having fun and talking about their various school adventures. Away from parents, I'm sure the jokes and teasing were in full swing and they were revealing things that they might not be inclined to tell their parents about. We've all had one of these weekends, with our old friends, regaling our new found freedom and feeling like we're really adults, right? And, given the epidemics running rampant during these years, I'm sure they also talked about their friends and who had been sick and who had also been married and such. It makes total sense, given it was 1961 and my mother was recently married, that at some point someone asked my mother if she was pregnant yet. My mother's response? As I've learned, she liked to have fun, had a good sense of humor and was with her best friends. So, naturally, her response was, "You might say I've been exposed." I love this more than I can even describe in words. I might be a little too old to say this, but my mom is a superhero!

Of all of the stories about my parents in those early days, one of my favorites is one my father told frequently. He described how they had reached his final year of college and Mom was living there, Jean was born and it was time to pay for that last semester rent on that lovely, but oh so tiny married unit apartment. As my father tells it, his scholarship covered tuition, but he had to cover rent and expenses. He spent several days wondering how he was going to pay for the semester of rent because they were nearly out of money. Thankfully, as he tells the tale, he received a tax return payment and it was just enough to cover the rent. He quickly took it to the office and paid for their housing and when he arrived home, he told my mother that he wasn't sure how they would eat, but they had a roof over their head. The reason I so love this story is because it succinctly tells the tale of my parents just figuring it out and making it through. My other most favorite story that is tied with the steak flying across the floor to the bathroom is that my sister Jean learned to walk in that tiny apartment. She was reticent back in the first year and my parents were trying desperately to get her to take her first steps. She also had a newfound love of Pepsi in the bottles they came in. It might have been the sweet flavor, but I suspect it was holding that retro bottle. In any case, a plan was hatched and they passed that pepsi bottle back and forth and Jean took her first steps in attempt to retrieve that bottle. Ingenuity at its finest! What I like about these stories is regardless of whether I heard them originally from Mom or Dad, when they are told they both smile. It's clear to me that they are fond memories and that my parents had fun just being together all their lives. As I think about this, again I curse the disease that is taking these smiles and memories from my mother, but I know, they live on in our tales, our reminiscing and here now, on these pages.

Eleven

⌒

The House, the Prom Dress, and the Castor Oil

Before that last year at Western, my mother and father were living in that upstairs apartment where Alice Lee had lived, where my mother's grandparents had lived and where cousin Gene McKay lived. My mother was pregnant with my older sister, their first-born child and the source of my mother's "exposure" (Yes, it's still funny!). My father was working various jobs, one of which was milk delivery early in the morning. My mother was shaking out rugs on the stoop of the house that was the entry for the upstairs apartment and fell off the stoop backwards. Grandma Floye, Linda and probably Cindy all went charging over to meet my mother at the hospital. Jean came early. Nearly a month early. In 1961, fathers were not in the delivery room. They waited outside the maternity ward in a waiting room and were told by a nurse their child had been born. My father was working when Jean was born. He came later and was told visiting hours were over. It was an entire day before he met his daughter. My mother told me some time when I was younger that she was told she might not be able to have more children because of that fall. That, she said, was why my name is Joy. Corny, I know, but I think it might have been the only "J" girl name they could come up with that made sense. I always wondered if perhaps my mother was "exposed" earlier than she claimed and that Jean might have been part of the reason for my parents' hasty elopement, but the story of the fall and rush to the hospital was corroborated by my aunts and grandmother, and that would totally not be in keeping with who I know my parents to be. Anyway, Jean was born just before my father's final year of college.

Jean later attended college at Western, but she had already been there. She lived in those married units with my parents. It is there that she learned to walk. She likely spoke her first words and there many laughs to be had as she did all those things little babies do. When I ponder this, I hear a baby's laughter, you know that full belly laugh that only babies have? I hope those memories are still there with my mother, perhaps they are, just not fully accessible to be retold at this point.

After graduating from Western Illinois University, my father gained employment as a math teacher at a fairly new high school up in the Chicagoland area. He also began a summer master's degree program at Indiana University a short time after he started teaching at Lake Park High School.

Three years later, as a teacher and coach and generally involved in a lot of supervisory tasks at the high school, my father was asked to chaperone the junior/senior prom. All of this would have been fine, if my mother hadn't been pregnant, with me. She was, and there was not enough money in the small budget of a teacher in the spring of 1965 to buy a maternity dress appropriate for a prom dance. So, my mother improvised. During high school, my mother had fabulous prom dresses. With her mother working at a dress shop, I'm sure they had the means and connection for these dresses. And, remember, there were a lot of homemade, sewn clothing in my mother's closet. My mother took one of those dresses and turned it into her prom chaperone dress. Sometime later, I found a picture of my parents from one of their proms, where she has a beautiful chiffon tiered-ruffle dress on. It had a flounce or petti-coat or something that makes it pouf out at the bottom and I think it was strapless. I always thought my mother looked classy and beautiful in that dress. Also, because of the elopement, and there being no wedding pictures, I always coveted that picture as a replacement wedding picture of my parents. Come to find out, I was in that dress too. My mother took that tiered-ruffled dress, added material under those tiers, and turned it into a dress she could wear while pregnant for her chaperoning assistance. So, I got to wear that beautiful dress, while resting comfortably inside my mother and dance at that prom before I was even born!

Here's that dress I love so much!

A month or so after that dance, my mother and my sister Jean went to stay with Grandma Floye for the summer because my father was attending class for his master's degree in Indiana. I've been told it was a very hot summer. Cindy was still at home, but by this time, Linda was married and living with my uncle Larry in that upstairs apartment. Each weekend, my father would drive over from Indiana and stay with my mother. As my arrival date approached, my father took time off of classes to stay in Chillicothe in case I decided to make an appearance. After a week, though, Dad had to get back to classes. Not before my mother tried just about everything she could think of to bring on labor. This included all kinds of tricks, and the one I am least excited to hear about, was her drinking nearly an entire bottle of castor oil. What is castor oil you ask? It is a thick, odorless oil made from the seeds of a castor plant. It has been used throughout history, first making an appearance in ancient Egypt as a lamp oil and later for medicinal purposes. Cleopatra thought it would whiten the whites of her eyes. It also is thought to induce labor. I say "YUCK". I know, she drank it, but remember, everything a mother puts into her mouth, the baby inside gets too.

My father left to head back to Indiana, and a full moon rose over North America, and overnight, either the moon or the castor oil or who knows what, and my mother went into labor. When this tale is retold at family gatherings throughout my life, this is where it gets really funny, as my Aunt Cindy had a mustang. It is reported, but this could be an extreme exaggeration, that she drove really fast, with my mother having labor pains and Grandma Floye holding on for dear life. They stopped, barely, at the emergency entrance of Proctor Hospital in Peoria and my mother was rushed in. I was born a few hours later and 5:13am. My father came rushing back from Indiana, having missed his second child's birth. I was named Joy Elizabeth. I share my middle name with my mother and grandmother. I gave it to my daughter and she in turn gave it to her daughter. Five generations of girls with Elizabeth as our middle names.

Over the next couple of years, we moved to an apartment near the high school where my father taught, and a few months after my birth, my older sister came home with the chicken pox. I got a very bad case of it. As my mother detailed in my baby book, I had chicken pox in my mouth, throat and ears. I also made friends with several little boys in the apartment complex and there are several lovely photos of me, belly sticking out, bikini clad, frolicking in a wading pool on the back stoop of the building.

As far as I know, my brother's birth two years later was not nearly as dramatic as the fall from the stoop at the apartment, nor the high-speed race through the back roads to Proctor hospital. I believe my father was present as his master's degree was completed. My brother carries a slight shift of my father's name, Jerrold and his middle name is Lee, after our mother, and her grandfather. Many years later, my youngest sister was peacefully born in Central DuPage hospital in Wheaton. Aunt Cindy came to stay with us while my mother was in the hospital. She taught us how to make egg sandwiches, with ketchup. I know it sounds kind of weird, but I still eat them this way, nearly fifty years later. Another new menu item while my mother was in the hospital delivering our baby sister to us, fluffernutter sandwiches. Those were my father's creation, made from peanut butter and marshmallow fluff. I don't eat those anymore, but I did all the way through college. You'd be surprised how filling two pieces of bread, peanut butter and marshmallow fluff from the jar can be, and how inexpensive they are for the poor college student.

When Jan was born, Jean and Jerry and I went to the hospital one night and we got to sit in the waiting room and see our baby sister on a closed-circuit television screen. Fathers were now allowed in the delivery room, but siblings were not allowed on the maternity floor yet. On the way home that night, Jerry asked if he could trade in all of his baseball cards, with this baby sister for a brother. I'm certain he was serious about wanting this trade and was already on his way at six years old to being a veritable savant about baseball and football statistics. So the trade of all of his baseball cards probably seemed like a gigantic sacrifice worthy of a sister for a brother swap. I think he might have had an inkling of what was to come sharing a house with three sisters and was hoping for a reprieve. When he was told by our father that trade was not possible, Jerry was condemned to grow up in a girl scout camp, as we frequently point out to him even now.

You'd say that Jan was a bit of an accident, but our family would not be complete without her. Jean and Jerry and I all look like our father. We have dark hair, dark eyes and the characteristic eyebrows of the Blew family. Jan is fair, like our mother was until she was in school. She retains her blonde hair, although now it is browner than it ever was. She has my mother's eyes and nose and being so much younger than us, has benefited from the most time with our parents. I envy her that now, especially now, when it seems each day, my mother loses more and more of these older memories and not just what she ate yesterday. I wonder if she remembers my rocking Jan to sleep at night as a baby, or how Jerry really wanted a brother.

Twelve

～

Jane's, the Rolltop Desk, and Shopping

After my grandfather died suddenly and left Grandma Floye to care for three girls, she went to work. I mean, they had to have money, right? I'm sure that was a daunting task in the early 1950's for a woman to go to work. There weren't many options for women. You could be a nurse, or florist, or a teacher, and I'm not sure there were many other options, especially in a town the size of Chillicothe, but she went to work at the local dress shop, Jane's. Jane's Dress Shop was located in downtown Chillicothe a few doors away from the Ben Franklin store. It had a big main floor room, a back room and an area of the store that was up a few stairs where all the really formal dresses hung. Whenever we would come to town and Grandma was working, we would stop in to Jane's to see her. I used to love to go into that store. It smelled like new clothes and cedar closets and Janet and I would frequently play hide and seek amongst those formal dresses. If we got into town near lunchtime, we would walk across the street and have sandwiches and burgers at the pool hall. Later, when I was a teenager and would go to visit Grandma in the summer, I would walk up to Jane's from her house and we would have lunch. She taught me on one of those trips to steam iron dresses. I loved to go there, and Grandma was always dressed so nicely, always appropriately accessorized, and always in her signature perfume, Channel. When I was little, Grandma would produce beautiful spring dresses, gloves and shoes to Jean and I for Easter. I loved those white gloves, and white shoes. Naturally, Grandma was with me when I went wedding dress shopping, and in point of fact, she picked out the dress I wore.

When we would go to Jane's or talk about it, my mother would describe how each year, they would prepare with new clothes from somewhere in Peoria, some dressmaker that provided clothing to Jane's or something. What I remember most were the rules. There were fashion rules. Your shoes, belt and purse must always match. You got out pastels at Easter and whites at Memorial Day and only winter white was worn after Labor Day. I think my mother inherited some of that fashion sense from her mother. First, she always followed the fashion rules. Also, she was always well dressed. I used to play in Grandma's walk-in closet. Later, I coveted the clothing in my mother's closet and was oh so disappointed when I could no longer wear her shoes. However, for a long time I benefited from my mother's ever changing career wardrobe and always had a selection of suits and dresses to rely on for my work wardrobe and whenever I had to dress up for a wedding or event.

As I have said a few times, we lived in the Chicago area, first in Itasca, then in Wheaton. You might not know where Itasca is, but Wheaton might be more familiar to people. It's where Red Grange, a famous football player is from, also where John Belushi is from, and where Billy Graham spent a lot of time. It was known for two things when I was growing up, having the most churches per capita for any town in America, and for being dry. We were the only part of my family on either my mother's or my father's side that moved away from central Illinois. So, we went back to Chillicothe a lot. We went back each year for Christmas Eve and Christmas Day, we would go back for family events, like birthdays, Aunt Cindy's wedding, to paint Grandma's house, and help people move to different houses. I started spending a week or so each summer down there when I was eleven or twelve and continuing until I was in college. Sometimes we went just to visit for the weekend or day, as it was only two hours from our house to Grandma's house.

Frequently, when my father was busy with football, wrestling, track or whatever, at Lake Park, my mother would take us all down to visit Grandma and her sisters. We would pile into the backseat of the car, argue over who had more space and play games on the two-hour drive. Mom would pull off of fourth street onto Sycamore and then into the alley that ran behind Grandma's house and into the gravel drive that ran between the one-car garage and the fire pit where they burned their garbage. We would clammer out of the car and up the stairs to Grandma's front door. On one such trip, Mom pulled onto the gravel drive and slammed the car into park and hopped out of the car. We probably all went flying forward in the backseat because there were no seat belts or car seats back then. Mom stopped suddenly and jumped out of the car because of what she saw Grandma Myrt doing. Grandma Myrt had two teenage boys standing nearby and she was partly standing in the fire pit, which was a cinder block enclosed on three sides approximately 36" high and about four feet by four feet inside area. Inside the firepit was the very large rolltop desk that had up until that day sat inside the office space of my great grandfather. Grandma Myrt had a small axe that likely came out of the one-car garage and she was chopping away at that nearly 100-year-old desk and had lit it on fire. My mother screeched at her in an attempt to get her to stop chopping, but it was already flaming up. There was no saving that desk.

Even at the young age that I probably was that day, I knew that a huge tragedy was occurring. I had played at that desk to be sure. But it was a part of my family history and even then, I appreciated the immense value of it purely as a family heirloom. In all the years since that day I have not seen another desk with such an impressive stature or made of such wood. Not to mention the prestige of that rolltop, the many drawers, and secret compartments with dove-tail finishing. My mother bemoaned that incident during that visit and nearly every other visit we made until Grandma Myrt could no longer distinguish between my mother and her sisters. We don't talk about it anymore, however, as my mother likely doesn't remember it. Every time I have gone to buy a desk, whether to outfit my office or for any of my children, I think of it.

The strongest women I know! Grandma Floye and her three girls

Clearly, my grandmother liked shopping. After years working in that dress shop, she could still run circles around all of us if the plan for the day was a shopping trip. My mother enjoyed a good day trip to the shopping malls, small town squares and outlet malls as well. We would often head off on a shopping adventure whenever Grandma or my aunts would come to town. We also generally planned a lunch and shopping in the summer in central Illinois in some small town. Our biggest two shopping events were just after Thanksgiving for our annual holiday gift-giving and a trip every summer to commemorate my mother's birthday. The Christmas shopping day was in November and started when Jean and my kids were little. We would gather at Mom's house and plan the day around stores where we knew we would find all the items on our list and would start by our sharing of gift ideas and planning what each of us was giving each family member. Then we would pile into cars and head out. After a few years, we included Linda and Cindy into this trip, which turned into more of a day of laughter than power shopping. We would walk around at least two entire malls, looking in windows and lugging bags around. A stop at lunch for some soup and salad and finish the day off with dinner.

The summer trip was more about getting together. We would drive Mom down to where her sisters lived and all of our female cousins would join. Again, we would have lunch at some little place and then wander through all the antique and specialty shops in whatever town square we ended up in. Like some families have a tradition of cooking and laying out huge spreads of food together, my mother's family goes shopping. It's where we gathered, exchanged stories, pictures and laughed all day.

I miss these trips. My grandmother is gone, my mother is not able to walk as much and has such a hard time with going places that we have stopped going on these trips. I miss them like I miss having my mother remember them.

Thirteen

~

Lake Michigan, Football Camp, and Pinochle

My father spent most of his adult life working at Lake Park High School. As a math teacher, coach and later as a principal. He spent his days with these teachers and coaches and over time, began spending time outside of school with these couples and as they all had kids, their families spent time with one another. In fact, many of my childhood memories are wrapped up with the children of men who taught and coached with my father.

One of those families is the Monkens. Mr. Monken was the head coach of the football team, while my father was the assistant coach. They had three boys that were close in age Jean and Jerry and I. Their boys were Tony, Todd and Ted. Look, another family with the same first letter thing! Anyway, with all that coaching going on, there was little time for family vacations. Generally, there were only a couple of weeks of the whole year when my father wasn't working on the football field, the wrestling mat or the track.

One year, the Monken's had rented a lake house on Lake Michigan and because of its size, invited us to go with them for a week in the summer. The parents all slept in rooms upstairs and the children were relegated to the basement, with the girls, Jean and I, in one room and all four of the boys, Jerry and the three Monken boys, in the other. We built all kinds of sand castles, swam in the lake and barbequed every day. One day, we all worked together and built an engineer's dream sand house. We scavenged the beach for chunks of wood to make seats and rocks to make tables. We played board games every night and listened to our parents laugh into the night.

One morning down in that basement, Jean woke up screaming. At some point in the wee hours of the beginnings of daylight, the Monken boys with the help of our little brother, found a frog and put it in Jean's bed with her still in it! Two sets of parents came running down the stairs and those boys were rolling on the floor of the basement laughing. My mother laughed, then quickly turned and hid her mouth so we couldn't see her smiling. She must have been thinking it was a great idea! Of course, Jean and I got even. I had no frog in my bed, but in solidarity with Jean, I helped to put some gross smelling wet thing from the beach between their sheets. I'm not sure they ever got the smell out of those sheets!

We shared many adventures with the Monken's, in fact. Several years after the frog incident it was decided that the wives and children of the football coaching staff would accompany the team on their summer training program to Indiana. The camp owner offered the house on the lake there to the wives and we loaded up and drove East to the Terry Cole Camp of Champions (I think that was its name?). A bit bedraggled when we arrived, we began cleaning that lake house with Mom and Mrs. Monken and after several hours of scrubbing stripped the sheets off of a bed and found all kinds of bugs crawling on the mattress. It was gross! Mrs. Monken and Mom announced we would not be staying. We spent the week at a hotel nearby with a pool, while the boys stayed in camp with the team and our father's. It was the last year we joined for football camp though. Mom had had enough, I guess.

Aside from these trips, my parents and other teachers and coaches at Lake Park at some point started a pinochle club. pinochle is a card game with 48 cards, but only pairs of cards from 9 to Ace. That's about all I know about that game. Each month or so, they would gather at one of their house's, and have dinner and play cards. Dinner was a pot luck kind of thing with the host providing the meat and everyone else bringing their assigned accompanying part of the meal. After dinner, the drinks would come out along with the cards. That is when, as a child, to my amazement, my parents and the adults that always seemed so serious were anything but serious. One of my father's co-workers would come and check on us kids when this event was held at our house and insist that we call him Cleetus. I'm certain this was not his first name, and never really knew what it was about, but he was funny, carrying his highball around and sneaking us food.

When this gathering was at our house, we were relegated to our rooms. We could come out to sneak around the back hall to the kitchen to get snacks and drinks, but we were not allowed to go through the living room where they had all the card tables set up. At this time in my mother's life, she liked amaretto stone sour drinks. I don't remember what my father's drink of choice was, but I think it was something whiskey related. Anyway, the only time I saw my father drunk was at these pinochle parties. And are my parent's funny when they're drunk! I know for certain and have known since I was that child watching in wonder at my father acting goofy that you should never ever let your kids know that you have been drunk or be drunk in front of them. You can never live that down. My mother, my mother has been three times that I can remember. The first time was at my best friend from high school's wedding. At that event, the bar was serving all kinds of shots. You know, the stupid ones with lots of sugar from the 80's. I thought it would be fun to see how my mother liked them and ordered her two or three. She was really funny and danced the night away. I learned the next day that she threw up in the Wendy's parking lot. The next time was at our son's graduation party. We practically planned this, as we had prepared a large cooler full of mai tai's and by this time, that was my mother's favorite drink. She didn't throw up but she was droopy eyed and silly by the time she left our house. The last time, about two years ago we were having dinner at my parent's favorite restaurant in Florida and my father had coupons for two for one margaritas. We were all talking and laughing and barely noticed that my mother with Alzheimer's had pulled her drink close to her and downed the first one in record time. We noticed when the waitress asked if she wanted another and she said sure. We controlled the drinking of the second one, but the damage was done. She could barely walk out of that restaurant that night. It was the last time she ever had an alcoholic drink.

These people that my parents socialized with were not just my father's co-workers and their wives, they were good friends. Friends that mother and father continued to have well after he retired and still keep in touch with to this day. While Mrs. Monken has recently had a stroke that really debilitated her, and Mr. Monken is suffering from Parkinson's, we still keep up with the teams Todd Monken has taken to national championships, and the goings on of all the children of Tony and Ted. We are still in contact with Jim and Heather Krupke, and know where they are moving to and what is going on in their lives. We prayed when children were sick, celebrated when jobs and promotions and military service occurred.

Mom enjoying a drink

But more than that, these people are weaved into my mother's life, through stories of digging out of snow storms, parties before any of them had kids, convention trips out west and a picture of my mother on the Hoover Dam. They have a comradery that spans decades and can gather after much time apart and talk as if they saw each other yesterday. It makes me really happy that although my mother devoted a lot of her life to raising her children, she still had fun, laughed, drank a little and had all of these people in her life. I doubt she remembers them at this point, but I hope she feels them and knows she was loved and cared for by so many.

Fourteen

꩜

Chores, the Garden, the pool, and All Those Christmas Decorations

When I was little, we had chores. It seems kind of foreign to most people to think about kids having responsibility to care for their home, but looking back, it taught us several things. First, to respect the home we share with others, to recognize and take our responsibilities seriously, and it was how I learned to do a lot of things. When it became age appropriate, we were allocated responsibilities around the house. That started with rotating on kitchen detail to set and clear the table, wash dishes and dry dishes. Yes, I did say wash dishes. This was before most people had dishwashers so each night, Jean and Jerry and I rotated jobs. As we got older, this phenomenon known as chores also included dusting and vacuuming the house, cleaning bathroom and kitchen, weeding the vegetable garden, emptying garbage and cutting the lawn.

It was a given in our house that all chores had to be done prior to play time. It was also a given that this was how allowance was earned. If you wanted money to buy candy at the nearby pharmacy, you had to do chores. If you wanted to buy lunch at school instead of making a lunch, you had to do chores. Other kids I knew growing up didn't all have the same set of chores. Some had similar chores, some different chores and of course, occasionally there was a friend that didn't have any chores.

In the heat of summer, I really didn't like the weeding chore, and every now and then I really disliked the dinner chores, but overall, I didn't really even think about it. Later, as I grew older I realized that some subversive learning took place on Saturday morning when we had to clean house before running out with our friends. I knew how to clean, knew how to get stains and pet issues out of all kinds of surfaces, knew how to grow my own vegetables, and more importantly, understood responsibility. Surprise, those seemingly inconsequential chores taught us a lot about life. I'm perfectly certain my parents knew exactly what they were doing. In fact, I used the same learning tactics on my own children when I became a parent. Something I now have full understanding of is that good parents, the ones that really help children to grow into great adults that accomplish anything, start small, telling their child to clean up their toys, make their bed and then do chores. Just as in being a great writer, sometimes the best path is to "show" instead of "tell". Show children how to be responsible instead of simply lecturing them on the importance of it.

Some time later, I was asked if my parents were somewhat abusive because of this constant ordering us to do things. I laugh at this. My parents weren't hard on us, and certainly not abusive, they gave us a precious gift. They taught us something that can't come in any other form, is not clearly spelled out in any textbook. It came from love, and came from their commitment to be parents. On this point, I know I have made it clear to my parents how thankful I am. I have told them that I appreciated what they taught me. Even if my mother can't articulate to me that I've previously thanked her, I know it's in there, somewhere hidden in her brain that can't always access the right information. I'm so grateful for everything she taught me and everything they gave me.

Now, I'd like to take a moment to expand on that garden chore. We had gardens. We have flowers in the front and down the side of our house and vegetables in the back. Each year, the marigolds had to be planted. The weeds had to be pulled the winter junk raked out of those flowerbeds. The vegetables were another story all together. The vegetable garden started out small. We always had tomatoes. But each year, Mom wanted to try something new so one year we tried to grow lettuce. That didn't work out so well. We had radishes, because Mom liked them. We usually had carrots, cucumbers and we tried beans one year too. The thing is, that each year, she decided it wasn't quite enough. There wasn't enough tomatoes or there wasn't enough carrots. So each spring we would have to dig out more grass in the back of the hard to make room for more garden. As the garden expanded, so did the task of watering in the spring to make sure all those plants grew, and then weeding all summer to make sure they flourished. Weeding is a terrible job. You are either bent over or on your knees. My turn to do this task was always on the clearest of days and definitely the hottest of days all summer.

All of this is why I was so glad when I arrived home from a summer visit with Grandma Floye and Nany to find that a decision had been made to put a pool in our back yard. The fact that we didn't really have time for vacations with all the sports teams of my father and my brother, made my parents decide to bring some of the fun to our backyard. The plus for me is that the garden had to shrink some. Also, I could wile away the hours floating on an inflatable raft in the pool. By the time the pool went in I was a teenager and my priority had become having the best possible tan all year round. In fact, one year, I made the find of the century in a catalog. It was an inflatable raft that was clear on the top and silver on the bottom. Jean and I located it and we ordered one. When I was a junior in high school, I was intent on advancing my tan early in the year and decided one warm day early in May that I would float on that raft. Grandma was up that weekend and she and my mother were heading out on a shopping day. They called to me from the driveway that I had best not fall asleep on that raft and left. Guess what? I fell asleep. The good news, the raft with the silver reflective bottom worked perfectly! The bad news, I was sunburned the whole length of my body. To paint a picture here, I was the color of one of our spring tomatoes from my hairline all the way down to my feet. That night I nearly passed out from the heat my skin was generating. Grandma had the perfect solution, though. I fought her the whole way, but in the end gave in and climbed into a tepid bathtub filled with water and an entire gallon jug of white vinegar. Here's a little secret, vinegar takes the sting out of any sunburn. Instantly. Now the redness didn't go away and by the end of the next week all my skin that had been the color of a tomato was now one continuous blister.

Despite the record-breaking sunburn, the pool was great. We had all kinds of parties out there, celebrated graduations and birthdays there, and my all-time favorite picture of my mother was taken during one of those pool parties. And, my mother liked to float the afternoon away too. Her love of the water and sun remained long after they moved from that house and headed south to Florida. She would sit for hours on the beach reading, working on her tan. Looks like another thing I have in common with Mom!

Still another thing I have in common with my mother is our love for Christmas decorating. All my expertise I learned from her. It started slow, or at least that's how my memory goes with this. We would set up a tree in our living room, Christmas pillows would come out, along with table linens for the season. Once my parents moved into their townhouse, after all but Jan had moved to their own homes, it started to grow. There were more trees set up, and those all started to have themes. She started collecting series of ornaments from Hallmark. That probably is the source of the themed trees, but she would buy the newest version of the Victorian houses, trains, and various Maxine decorations for the tree. Then, the Santa and snowmen collections started. I'm not sure if that began with my aunt Linda or my mother, but it proved to be a great idea as it offered gift ideas galore. My mother and her sisters would exchange gifts each year and more often than not they were to add to these collections.

One of our happy Christmas celebrations

The result of all of these collections is that all rooms in the house started to have some sort of decorations for the Christmas season, if only to have a place to display them all. The collecting spilled out to my sisters and I, and my cousins, because we too wanted our homes cheerfully expressing the love of the season. It got pretty serious one year when my son and nephew decided to start counting all the Santa's at each person's house to determine who the big winner was. Between my mother and her sisters and my two sisters and I, we determined in our family we have over 500 Santa figures, and over 200 snowmen decorations! I'm not sure there are any left to buy really. Because last year I was searching for a new Santa for my mother to spark her memory of this beloved family tradition and I could not find one that I didn't think one of us already owned.

The years went by and my parents began an effort to downsize their belongings and several of these collections were deeded to my sisters and I. This only added to my number, it certainly not the beginning of my collecting. In fact, the last year my kids were all in one spot with us for Christmas, my son again counted them and I had gotten dangerously close to breaking 100. My middle son's response to this feat? "It looks like Christmas threw up in here." So now, each year, as the Thanksgiving weekend winds down, this very thoughtful son will contact me and ask if Christmas is throwing up yet. Lovely, huh?

We still decorate at Mom's house. She doesn't do much of the work, my sisters and I do the setup, but she does sit in her chair and tell us where to put things. We've actually started taking pictures each year so we can be sure to put everything just where it had been placed in previous years. Unspoken between us all is the knowledge that maintaining this tradition for her and the placement of everything being consistent helps to keep that memory fresh and make her comfortable. We do a lot of things now to keep her comfortable.

I hope someday, my children will take up this tradition. I would like to show up at one of my kid's houses and be greeted by grandchildren and have them pull me room to room, ending at their rooms to show me their special tree and decorations. Even if it means my grandchildren will someday blame me for this excess, I know deep down, this will be a memory for all of us for many generations.

My decorating you ask? I'm down to two trees really. One that has my family collection of ornaments. Those that my kids picked out, and made through the years. The ones we've added when my son-in-law joined the family to pay homage to his Marine status, the zoo animals' ornament when our youngest found his love, the cardinal ornament painted for me. This is my special family tree. The other, in homage to my mother, is a themed tree. Now that I live close to the beach, it is beachy Christmas tree. Some of my Santa collection doesn't come out anymore. I've started to collect beachier Santa's, rather than the arctic collection I've acquired. To be sure, Christmas does still throw up at my house, but now, I have more important things to worry about. We have to care for my mother and help my father. Alzheimer's has taken this from us.

Fifteen

~

Christmas, the Money Tree, and the Shoes

So, it's clear Christmas is important to my family. It has always been a time to gather and laugh and share. It was, for many years total chaos. Remember, my parents were the only members of both of their families to move away from central Illinois. When I was younger, this always meant we returned to the family homebase, in Chillicothe. The problem for us, being the ones that travelled most years, was that we were kids and wanted those gifts. You know, we looked through the Sears Christmas catalog and selected all the toys, clothing and things we thought we absolutely had to have, and circled them, folded down pages and hoped that we would get everything on our list. You know you did it too. Admit it.

This presented a problem, however, because we couldn't drag all those gifts with us to Chillicothe each winter. We were carrying gifts for cousins, grandmothers and such. So each year, my immediate family celebrated Christmas a week or so before the actual date at our house. A plan would be concocted by my parents for one of them to get all four of us out of the house for a short period of time. Sometimes it was as simple as meeting my father for dinner and he going straight home while we stopped for something. Other times it was more elaborate with the neighbors sometimes being involved to play Santa for us. Upon our arrival home, Santa would have visited our house. Why someone would always ask, did Santa come just to us early? Well, as the story goes, Santa knew we had to drive to Chillicothe for Christmas and so he came early so we could enjoy our gifts before we had to leave. That was generally enough and we would tear into the gifts and have a day or two to glory over them before we had to leave.

The trips to Chillicothe were always an adventure. I mean it was Christmas in central Illinois. Snow would be falling; wind would be howling and we frequently were alone on the roads. As I've explained earlier, this usually meant arguing in the back seat over who had more room on the seat, or playing the alphabet game, which was rather hard on state roads with few road signs. These trips always began on the afternoon of Christmas Eve. In all the years we made that trip, I can only remember two times when we were allowed to stop on the way. The first was when we had a new dog, Pudgie, and he had to go to bathroom. We stopped on some lonely and snow filled stretch of road and he scampered off to find a place to go when he disappeared in the white out of snow blowing around. The snow as deep and he was white. It took us several minutes to find him and rescue him from a snowdrift. The other was when I was in my teens and had a terrible upset stomach. My father relented and allowed us to stop before we got onto the highway so I could use the bathroom.

We would arrive at Grandma Floye's house and bound up those stairs with the gifts and things. Grandma's house was the place we celebrated Christmas with my mother's family. When everyone had arrived, we would have dinner and open gifts. Some important rules to these celebrations. First, we always had tortellini for dinner with carrot cake for dessert, and gifts were always opened from youngest to oldest. Back when I was younger, everyone got gifts from everyone. Three sisters, their husbands and seven children, along with Grandma Floye and Grandma Myrt. It took all evening to get through all those gifts! Then, after all the paper was cleared away and all the gifts loaded into the car, we would make our way to Nany's house. It was usually after nine at night when we got down there, but faithfully, there was a kitchen table loaded with plates of cookies and things and Nany would always allow us to have a treat before we went to sleep. Before my grandfather passed away, Jean and Jerry and I would sleep upstairs in the big room that had been my dad and his brother's room. In the morning, my grandfather would come to the bottom of those stairs and

One of those lovely Christmas outfits

yell "Ho, Ho, Ho!" Naturally we would all wake up and this would be the start to the family Christmas with my father's side of the family. We called my grandfather PawPaw. He always sat in a big red chair and smoked a pipe. Nany would begin breakfast preparations and someone would call my father's sister and brother to tell them to get up and get down there. We would anxiously await their arrival so we could eat breakfast. Now, in case I hadn't already told you, my grandparents were from Missouri. From generations of family on farms. This is helpful to know as our breakfast for Christmas morning looked something like a bunk house breakfast. Fried eggs, ham, biscuits and gravy, and the best part, homemade bread, toasted, with honey butter. Again, after everyone was full from the breakfast feast, we would all gather in the living room and pass out gifts. After all the gifts were opened, and paper cleared, we often would pile into the cars and our uncle would take us to the school where he was a science teacher and basketball coach so we could run around and play in the gym. When we returned, we would eat again.

As the years passed, some of this ritual celebrating began to change. First, we decided sixteen or eighteen people opening gifts was not really the point to the day so we started drawing names. Everyone still got something, but we greatly reduced the time spent opening and the cost associated with gift giving in a large family. Later, we decided only the kids would get gifts, and the grandmothers. That meant another reduction in the gifts and costs. Eventually, as my generation grew up and married and had kids, the gifts started to become cards with money and after Grandma Floye passed away, we basically stopped doing gifts at all, preferring to just have the event about spending time together. Now that my parents, Jean, Jan and I live away from Illinois, we don't really get the chance to do this celebrating anymore. Taking Mom on a road trip is a big project. We don't do it very often and she couldn't fly now. It would be too much on her. Plus, now other members of my family are getting older and travel is harder for everyone. This is the saddest part about Alzheimer's to me. It's robbed us all of this very special gathering tradition. I can still see my mom and her sisters laughing in the kitchen, and mom smiling with delight over her tennis bracelet. I am now the keeper of the homemade bread and honey butter recipe that my Nany so famously is known for. I make sure to make enough for everyone when we gather, but I sure wish we all could go back there. I'd really like to see my mom dressed up in her holiday outfit and laughing with her sisters.

The other big thing that happened in our family at Christmas was an ingenious idea my great-grandmother Myrt came up with. She, I'm sure, got tired of trying to figure out what to get all her granddaughters, their husbands and her great-grandchildren so she found this very gaudy white and maybe silver tipped table top Christmas tree. To it she tied an equal amount of money for each of us in bright red ribbon to the branches. The first year she rolled this out, she must have kept the tree hidden somewhere because I don't remember seeing it until she brought it out just after dishing up her oversized portions of dessert. I might have been around ten years old at the time. Grandma Myrt made a big show of untying those ribbons and handing out money to each of us. By the next year, my brother and sisters and cousins were ready and somewhere in there this tree was renamed the money tree. This money tree was perfect as far as I was concerned. We had already had Christmas and I already knew what I wanted and didn't receive and this gave me a chance to get that one thing I didn't already get. For one day, at least, Grandma Myrt was the hero. All of this seemed very incongruous to my great grandmother's miserly style of managing her money, but I know, at least, I didn't question that much when there was money to be had from that tree.

One year, we decided before we even made the trip that we were going to pool our money and get another television. The money Grandma

Myrt gave us all would be enough to purchase a new tv. We loved the idea. I wasn't even bothered about not getting to spend the money on the gift I didn't get, because this meant when my parents had pinochle we had a tv to watch because Dad assured us we could take this portable tv into our room to watch tv. Yes, it was a portable tv. It probably wasn't as big as most monitors are today, but we all felt like we were a big deal. We had that tv for a long time. I ended up taking it to college. I didn't have it on much, except on Sunday afternoons to have football games on tv in the background while I studied. I found it really hard to concentrate without that tv on, and John Madden's voice announcing the Sunday game. I don't remember what happened to that television. Maybe Jerry took it to Texas for school, or maybe it died a peaceful death in Wheaton. When we had to put Grandma Myrt in a nursing home, someone brought out that lovely white table top tree and we laughed about it. It still had some red ribbon on it. No one wanted to take it home, I remember. That was the end of the money tree.

Each year Mom would get a new Christmas outfit to wear to these celebrations. It always had some red in it, but some years it was skirt, some years it was pants. The big part of the outfit, was the new shoes. Mom loved shoes. When I was growing up, at some point, Mom had so many shoes that she had to pack up winter shoes during summer to have all her summer shoes out and then pack up summer shoes to get the winter shoes out. They were in boxes, labeled on the side, handing on the back of her closet door and on shoe racks on her closet floor. There were shoes wherever she could tuck them. And she had great shoes. It seemed like she had a different pair of shoes for every outfit. We did, in fact, make fun of her shoes most of the time, even as I coveted them. She had so many black shoes, one time I think we might have counted over 15 pairs of black shoes.

I wonder if her love of shoes came from her coveting her Aunt Elma's strappy shoes when she was younger? Anyway, when I was just starting high school, I was in heaven because Mom and I wore the same size shoes. Don't think for a minute that she let me borrow just anything from her closet. It was a very big deal when she allowed me to wear her shoes. Alas, it didn't last long because by the time I was 16 I could no longer wear her shoes. My feet had grown two sizes bigger than Mom's. It was heartbreaking, to be sure. When she retired from working and my parents started spending half of the year in Florida, she traded in her fancy black pumps and loafers for sandals. She has lots and lots of sandals!

Obviously, there is a gene for shoes on each person's DNA. Some are happy with two pairs of shoes; some have to have closets full of them. My mother was of the second type. I, fortunately inherited this gene from her. Although I spent many years teasing my mother about why someone needs 15 pairs of black shoes, I have found in this case, the pot did call the kettle black. I have at least 10 pairs of black shoes right now in my closet. So it must go on, as my boys are convinced I can't walk by a display of flip flop sandals without buying some. I must confess that one year, while on spring break, I did buy four pairs of flip flops. Perhaps, then, this teasing I receive is accurate on some level.

My family has joked for many years about our genes. Those we have inherited from our parents and those we like and don't like. For instance, we all wish we had my father's teeth genes, he didn't have a single filling until he was in retirement. We wish we didn't receive the gout, kidney stones and bad eyesight, and we all wish we had inherited a little more of the height gene from Uncle Tony. In my case, I'm delighted to have inherited the shoe gene. I hope I honor it well in my lifetime and do my mother proud. Even now we work to make sure she has the right shoes on with each of her outfits.

We try to honor her love of shoes now that Dad and my sisters and I are managing the purchasing of clothing for Mom. We try to find cute slip-on shoes and sandals to match all of her outfits. She may not remember that she loves shoes, but we do. They're slip-on now because it's just easier when we're trying to help her get dressed to have her put her feet into these shoes. No more laces for her. But her looks are always polished. Just how she would have wanted it.

Sixteen

∾

Concerts, Drum and Bugle, and the JC Penny Incident

My mother clearly loved music her whole life. I can remember watching Elvis on TV with her when I was young girl. She would play records while she did things around the house. I grew up hearing Elvis, Patsy Kline, Frankie Vallie, and later Neil Diamond, and Garth Brooks. I could probably karaoke every Neil Diamond song still, that's how often they were played at my house. At the time I probably gave my mother all kinds of crap about her choice in music. Now, they seem like old friends and a link to my mom. I tried to be musical. My pick was not the trombone; however, it was a string instrument. Yes, as a lefty, playing the violin is harder, but that was my choice. Of course, it didn't help that the instructions for playing the violin were "here's how to do it as a right-handed person, just do everything in reverse." Needless to say, it was hard. The hardest part, understanding that reverse thing while trying to master the pressure of the bow. Needless to say, my mother referred to my efforts as horrible scratching. I didn't play very long.

This traumatic experience did not deter my love of music. As we got older, and determining what gifts to give our mother for Mother's Day and birthdays became much harder. I assume this is true for everyone, but this love of music showed us a way to give her something memorable and something we knew she would always enjoy. We took her to concerts. We started with the easy one, Neil Diamond. Thankfully, he visited Chicago almost every year and we went a couple of times. Then, we moved on to Garth Brooks. That allowed my mother to invite sisters, nieces and her oldest granddaughter. Yes, she was the coolest aunt and grandmother. This proves it. After we ran out of concerts she would want to see, we started taking her to Broadway productions. I've seen Cats, Wicked, and Jersey Boys as a celebration with my mom, my sisters and my aunts and cousins. We laughed all the way to and from these events, and enjoyed some really great theater and concerts. Naturally, they are also sources of some family fun memories. My daughter's first concert, prior to middle school, I might add, was Garth Brooks with Grandma for her birthday. She hated it. It was too loud and I spent most of that concert listening from the hallway outside. We still point out that it was the most expensive t-shirt I ever bought. The ticket to get in, the show I didn't really see and then that t-shirt my daughter decided she absolutely had to have while spending an hour in the hallway. Jersey Boys? That was the day that I saw my mother, and both of her sisters singing and dancing through most of a Broadway show. The music being that of their younger years, but it was still funny to see them acting more like teens than the mothers of all of us there.

When I was growing up, fourth of July celebrations in Wheaton, IL were those of quintessential middle America. We had days of events each year. There was a parade on morning of the fourth, marked by Shriners in little go carts, dressed up and wearing those hats with the tassels. The bands from all the area high schools and of course, because it is Illinois, the politicians trying to get noticed by their constituents. I even marched in that parade a couple of times. Once twirling a baton, the three miles of the parade route, and once as member of a girl scout troop. Yes, I am a celebrity, well not really, but did march in the parade. There were fireworks, of course and the little league playoffs always coincided with the fourth weekend. I was at that several years, as a spectator. That particular celebrity belongs squarely with my brother, who thought he was responsible for carrying the undedicated, untrained, or not quite passionate players sharing the field with him. The best part of the festivities, by far, was the event that launched the town's celebration. The drum and bugle corps competition. Not everyone in my family appreciated this event, but my mother and I almost always attended. She, being a long-standing member of the marching band, wanted to see the best of the region playing. I just really loved the whole music and marching and coordinated movement around the field. Some years, Grandma Floye came up for the holiday and then we would all go. Later, cousins and other members of the family ended up playing in some of these competitions.

What I really loved about these was the coordinated marching around the field and the sheer sound of all those instruments together. It sometimes gave me chills. I'm sure it was the same for my mother, because she smiled through the whole thing every year. I don't know if they still do this in my hometown, but I know I haven't seen one of these drum and bugle corps since I was in college. The memory of sitting in those bleachers watching the bands makes me smile even now. I'd really love it if I could find one and get my mother to it. I know she'd enjoy it, even if she can't remember when we used to go every July 3rd.

As memories of my childhood go, my mother always seemed so mild-mannered and was very slow to anger. I don't remember ever seeing her get filled with anger for another person other than when we misbehaved. It was a real surprise to me to learn of her getting heated by someone, but the reason for my mother's anger seems like something I would expect of her. Her loyalty for her family is something I never questioned of my mother.

My father's younger sister married after my parents had moved to Chicago for my father to teach at Lake Park High School. When my aunt, whom we all know as Aunt Kay, was newly married and living in her first small place, my mother decided that she would like to help her make her new home feel more like home and offered to bring down her sewing machine and make curtains. Down she drove and while Aunt Kay was working my mother went to JC Penney to buy fabric. In those early days of the 1960's department stores had a little bit of everything. Kind of like a walk-in Amazon. You could get your hair done, pick out a new outfit, including shoes and a purse, buy birthday cards, dishes, towels and sheets. And, they had a sewing department where you could buy patterns, fabric and all the notions to make anything from a wedding dress to Halloween costumes. When it was my mother's turn at the cutting counter to get the fabric, she needed measured and cut, the woman working the counter asked what the fabric was for. This was probably just friendly small talk and a way for one crafty person to interact with another crafty person. When my mother explained that she was there to get fabric to make new curtains for her sister-in-law who had recently married, the nice lady behind the cutting counter at JC Penney began a tirade about her new daughter-in-law. She obviously didn't like this new daughter-in-law and was not afraid to tell customers, who were complete strangers. When this woman mentioned the ungrateful daughter-in-law's name, my mother realized that she was talking about Aunt Kay. The woman had no idea who my mother was, but my mother was instantly and intensely full of anger for this woman. She pushed the bolts of fabric across the counter and announced she could keep her miserable fabric and without informing her that her daughter-in-law was my mother's sister-in-law, she turned and marched out of the JC Penney.

My mother, in case you're wondering, did finish those curtains for Aunt Kay. She announced, still angry about it hours later, that she would get the fabric back in Chicago and get them all sewn up and bring them down the next week. Why she didn't tell that woman that the daughter-in-law she was complaining about was in fact the same woman my mother was sewing the curtains for, I'm sure I'll never know. I'm pretty sure the only reason I heard this story at all was because I had questioned Aunt Kay about her stories and memories of my mother.

It warms me up to know that my mother was ready for a fight to protect someone in her family. Warms me because that's how I am. My kids used to refer to me as Momma Bear. I'm pretty sure it's because I didn't keep a story like this about me from my kids. They may have even witnessed me acting in this protective manner once or twice. In that, the label is justified, although perhaps a trifle inappropriate. I know that's why I didn't hear this story from my mother. She was always very careful about sharing her past when it showed her as being tempted by or acting in a way that she had preached to us about. She was very proper that way. She would certainly tell you if you asked, which is how I learned about the flyswatter, the castor oil, the chicken pox and several other stories. But you had to know what to ask and how to ask to get my mother to tell her stories. Once we were all adults, she seemed to open up more, but when we were kids, we had no idea our mother was this funny, feisty and protective. Well, except for one incident.

When I was in sixth grade, Jerry was in fourth grade. There was a kid in my class that had a younger brother in Jerry's class. I don't remember that younger brother's name, but I remember he was kind of bully, wanting to fight and push people around. One day while walking back to school from lunch (yes, we went home for lunch in elementary school because our house was less than a block away from the school), that younger brother pushed Jerry into the street in front of the school. Now generally, there were very few cars rolling through our neighborhood. Less during the day, but if there were cars, they were near the school with mothers dropping kids off. Fearing for my brother, laying in the street, I first pulled him back onto the sidewalk and then turned to this younger brother and pushed him against the kindergarten play yard fence, hard. My brother then proceeded to punch him in the gut. All afternoon in class, Chris, the older brother that was my age was bragging how he was going to beat the crap out of my brother for hitting his brother. He had no interest in learning my or any other witness's retelling of the events that made his brother responsible for starting this little incident.

Wanting to protect my brother, I went through the library when the afternoon bell rang and collected him by his third-grade room and walked out the front door of the school hoping to avoid Chris. He was waiting there for us. He came at my brother and in one move, I pushed my brother behind me and shoved Chris and fell, sprawled out on the sidewalk. With kids gathered around us, now laughing, we drew the attention of the office staff and were told to break it up and go home. Jerry and I walked home and told our mother what happened and by the time we finished with our tale, Chris, his brother and his mother pulled into our driveway. Where, and no surprise here, their mother proceeded to scold and yell at my mother for raising such children that were picking fights.

My mother was having none of this. She told this agitated mother that her kids wouldn't get punched and pushed if they weren't trying to pick on others and perhaps the lesson that day was that they should stop that lest they run up against someone that was stronger than they were. This made Chris' mother angrier and who knows what would have happened. We will never know because at that moment my mother shut the door in their faces. I'm certain I smiled at that, but deep down, I was worried what was going to happen to me now that I had admitted to pushing Chris and Jerry had admitted hitting his brother. My mother turned from that closed door and said she hoped they didn't sit out there long and asked if we wanted a snack before we started homework. I must have looked astonished. My father never heard about what happened that day, at least not in my presence. No one got in trouble at our house, which I had been certain was coming. My mother was Momma Bear that day! I never told her this, but she became my hero that day. Even now, I get all warm thinking about how I always knew she would protect me.

Of course, now, the tables have turned and I feel like it's my job, with my sisters and brother, to protect her. When she gets scared about where we are, or anxious about walking somewhere or going to the doctor, I reassure her, telling her that nothing will happen to her while I'm there.

No one will get to her. She smiles at me when I say that. I hope she understands what I understood that day. She is protected. I hope Alzheimer's doesn't take that from her.

Seventeen

❧

Popcorn, Pudgie and Jordan

A long time ago, when Jerry was two years old, we were at the Monken's house. I don't remember if our father's were there or if they were out scouting some football team or having some meeting, but Jean, Jerry and I were there playing with Tony, Todd and Ted. We were in their backyard on their swingset. They had a swing on their set that was two seats facing each other and slats for a floor for people to get into and out of those seats. While we were pushing each other, two outside the swing pushing and four of us sitting on the seats, the older kids were hooking their feet under those floor slats rather than holding on to show how cool we were. Jerry, being the smallest there, had to try this of course, while Jean and Tony were pushing. The swing went way up and then came down and the force of that coming down pulled Jerry out through the opening between the seat slats and the floor slats. This pulled his leg and broke it, but at the time we didn't know that. We just knew he was hurt. I was told to run and get Mom.

I ran inside and up to my mother, who was talking with Mrs. Monken and some other adults. Naturally being taught not to interrupt, I did a dance there next to my mother waiting for an opportunity to break into that conversation and tell her Jerry was hurt. Finally, someone noticed me and I breathlessly told them Jerry was hurt. Al the adults ran outside and found Jerry laying on the ground with Jean and Tony next to him. His leg not looking like it was pointing in the right direction. This was our first trip to Central DuPage Hospital. Jerry did, in fact, break his leg, in several places. He was in a cast, that went all the way down one leg, covered his hips and partway down the other leg. I don't know if this was due to the severity of the breaks or just the fact that it was 1969. He was going to be in that cast all summer long.

This summer spent indoors is what brought my parents to the decision to get a dog. There was another teacher at Lake Park whose wife bred and showed shelties. She had a litter that had what her assessment was a runt. She offered the runt to my parents and that was how we got our first dog. Jerry got the honor of naming her and because his favorite food at that time might have been popcorn, and she looked like a burnt piece of popcorn, she was named, you guessed it, Popcorn. Popcorn was a gentle, beautiful dog. I don't remember if she did in fact keep Jerry company that summer, but she became mostly my dog. She would lay with me and sit by me while I read books or drew. Later, that breeder tried to buy her back from my parents because she had become the best-looking dog of that litter. We didn't sell her back. Some years later, while I was spending a couple of weeks in Chillicothe with my grandmothers, mom came down to get me and brought Popcorn's dishes to give to Linda. I was devastated and mad at my mother for a long time over what I saw was a total betrayal of my connection to this dog. However, Popcorn had developed stomach cancer and had stopped eating while I was away, and in fact, my mother was trying to save me the heartache of having that dog go to the veterinary office and not come out.

A couple of years later, I had begun watching the pets of the next-door neighbors while they vacationed. I liked their dogs and cat and more importantly, I was interested in earning some money by then. Mr. Rogeist, that neighbor, was a construction worker. One day, he came over to our house and told me someone had abandoned a box full of puppies and he had brought one of them home. His wife was not happy and he asked me to take this poor, under-nourished white fluff ball. I said I doubted my father would let me and he suggested in his usual fashion that it was better to ask for forgiveness than permission. I probably laughed and allowed him to leave the dog with me. When my mother got home, she fell in love with the little thing and I thought ok, I was getting a dog. Then my father got home. I had already reached a point where I was going to have trouble giving up this little fur ball, so holding my breath, I told him in as tragic a method as I could the tale of abandonment. My father grumbled that we didn't have the time to take care of another dog, but then an interesting thing happened. That little white fur ball jumped up onto the ottoman of my father's chair and sat, looking directly at him. I, as a final plea, repeated the words Mr. Rogeist had told me about forgiveness over permission and my father gave the dog a Cheeto. He smiled over Mr. Rogeist's words and then asked what this dog's name was. In that instant, I called him Pudgie, because he was anything but. Thus began our adventure with our second dog. Pudgie was for sure my dog. He slept with me, anxiously waited for me at the end of the day, and did live up to his name and become pudgie from all the food we gave him, and all those Cheetos that my father fed him. He was the dog we nearly lost in the snow on the way to Chillicothe for Christmas one year. Being white, and the drifts being large, he fell into one and was nearly lost. He too lost his life to cancer. This time, intestinal.

After I had moved out and gotten married, Jan started working after school and between years at college at a store that was right next door to a pet store. One day she called my mother from work and asked if she would come over at the end of Jan's shift and go see a dog at this pet store. This little yorkie stole both my sister and my mother's heart and after deciding to split the cost of this pet, he came home with Jan. Again, Dad was not consulted and arrived home to find a new dog in the house. Again, he gruffly approached the prospect of another dog and grumbled about it until the little dog jumped up on the ottoman again and it was instant attachment on both their parts. Yes, my father fed this dog Cheetos too. Jan named this dog Jordan, after Michael Jordan. He was cute and playful and had a very friendly disposition. Jordan passed from old age and deteriorating bones.

Although my parents never got another dog, they did provide babysitting services for both Jan's and my dogs later on. Tucker, Jan's westie, and Jenna, my sheltie mix, spent some time at Grandma and Grandpa's house. They both even visited during spring break trips to Florida. And yes, my father fed them Cheetos.

I don't know if my parents ever talked about having dogs when they talked about having kids. If Jerry hadn't had that broken leg, would we ever have gotten our first dog? Who knows? My mother certainly loved all those dogs we've nurtured and cared for. I did get over the anger of losing Popcorn, not blaming my mother for the choice she made to humanely end her suffering that summer I was away. Dogs have played an important role in our family. In fact, at one point my own son declared that Jenna and Grandma had to live forever. I know he knows that's not possible, but I totally understand the sentiment. They are both very important to me too and hope I don't have to face either of their passing any time soon.

Eighteen

༄

Lake Park High School, Track Finals, and Trips to CDH

Shortly after my father graduated from Western Illinois University, my parents, along with Jean, moved north so that my father could join the teaching staff at Lake Park High School. My father was a math teacher and coach for all the years my siblings and I were growing up. Why include this here in a book about my mother? Well, we all spent a lot of time there. It was the source of the family income until Jan was in school all day. And it's where I went to prom while my mother was pregnant with me, and where we spent nearly every weekend of our lives.

Because we were always there when the students were not, the school was a mysterious place for me when I was growing up. The lights were off, the halls quiet, and we played hide and seek in the teachers' offices and classrooms. When we got a little older, we would play in the gyms, and my favorite was the practice gym for the gymnastics team. Playing on the balance beam, uneven bars, rings, horse and, of course, the trampoline were great ways to pass an afternoon. My father's desk was always orga- nized, while some teachers were rather messy at their desks. He had a metal file cabinet that for years bore a small newspaper clip of an oak tree and a small sapling with the words, "What did the small sapling say to the big oak tree? Gee, I'm a tree!" Yes, it was a math joke, and it always made me smile.

A few times a year, we would all go over to the school on Sunday to do team laundry and sorting. This involved matching up knee pads and hip pads and such that were all numbered. As players returned them after the season, they would be matched, checked and stored away for the next year. Then jerseys and pants and wrestling singlets would be washed and dried in this weird room that was part janitor room, part team supplies where the washer and dryer were located. Yes, you're correct in thinking we were kind of captive labor. But during the season, we would pack up the warm clothing and mom would drive us from our home to Lake Park and we would watch high school football, and the band at halftime. Jerry would make his way to the field to help or just stand around the team and feel important. Jean and I would meet up with the Krupke kids, or later, sit with the high school kids and cheer on the team. I may not have been watching those games closely, but I was paying some kind of attention because later, in college and even as an adult, I could pick out penalties and see blitzes before some of my male friends.

During wrestling season, we would pack up for the whole day and sit in the gym. Jean would sometimes get volunteered to help with the record keeping of the matches, and Jerry usually got drafted to run timers and flip point flags. I did little during these days but read books I brought with me or help my mom entertain Jan for the long day. Then, during track season, we would all get drafted to help. I frequently was at the long jump/triple jump pit to measure in the sand. Jerry would track laps and run timers, and Jean would gather stats. So, it might be said that Lake Park was a family affair for us, with mom playing the role of organizer, driver and general supporter. A role she carried well, both during this phase of our lives and later when she was watching Jerry, Jan and I at sporting events of our own, and keeping everything running in our house.

Ok, this is not Lake Park, but I love this
picture of my Mom at a military museum
holding this gun!

The best part for me at Lake Park was when we watched the band, or went back to Lake Park for the plays, musicals, and things. I loved watching the marching band and sitting in the auditorium watching the chorus or plays. When Jan was very little, we went to a Christmas program at Lake Park on Friday night. On the way home, a student who was angry with my father tried to run us off the road. We ended up in a deep ditch along Medina Road. The back door was mangled to where it wouldn't fully shut anymore and it got cold in the car quickly. Two other teachers, I think maybe the Monken's or the Pasquini's, were behind us and saw the kid side swipe us. They took off after him. Another car pulled over to wait with us and someone went and called the police. This was way before cell phones, so we were stuck there for a long time waiting for someone to find a pay phone, call the police and for the police to arrive. Luckily, although it was a cold ride home, we could drive the car away from there once we were pulled out of the ditch. That was a scary night. Mom was cool as a cucumber. I don't know how she did that. She kept Jean and

Jerry and me from panicking in the back seat, all the while keeping Jan warm. She might have been scared, but I never saw that. That's how she always was. Cool and calm.

Over time, the school district grew, and they built another high school. My father moved to that other campus and became the head of the math department. That didn't last for long and they moved him to an administrative job. He became the vice principal. Then he moved back over to the older campus and became the principal. Some years after his retirement, we were back at that school when my daughter was playing tennis in high school. Of course, my young son had to use the bathroom, so we went inside the building. It had changed so much! I wasn't sure where to find the restrooms, where years before I could find my way around that building in the dark. Of course, thirty years had passed, so what was I expecting? A janitor approached us and I identified myself. Well, I identified myself as Jerry Blew's daughter, because I saw a plaque on the wall to his honor, and I hoped that would hold some weight for my illicit entry to the school. Guess what? It did! The janitor remembered my father. He took us directly to the faculty lounge and when my son was finished; he let him get some candy from the machine in the lounge and we returned to the tennis match.

At the end of every track season, usually right around Memorial Day weekend, they held the state championships at a college in central Illinois. We went almost every year because my father worked that track meet. Jean and I spent most of the time working on our tan on the hot, but reflective, shiny silver bleachers. Jerry followed Dad around. Every once in a while, Lake Park would have a few track athletes qualify for this meet and then my father scrambled around to help with the running of the meet and be these guys' coach. The only year I can remember we didn't go along was when I was a sophomore in high school and I had a date to the prom. It was a big deal for me, and for Mom, as I was the first of us kids to go to prom and we went shopping for a dress, and did all the preparation. It was fun dress shopping with Mom. I had my hair done. That didn't turn out and the lovely updo that I wanted fell apart in the warm, humid afternoon. I ended up restyling it at that last minute.

Anyway, that was probably the last year we all tagged along for the state track finals. I'm not sure if mom appreciated that change or not. She seemed to take all the Lake Park activities in stride. Later, she revealed that in fact, she sometimes didn't like all the driving, games, meets and events. I remember hearing that and thinking about how she never gave that away. She never let on that she didn't want to do all those things. It made me wonder about two things. One, why she didn't speak up, and two, what would she rather have been doing? It's funny, isn't it, that some parents seem to be so focused on that task that they stop doing things they love to do? Later, my mother took up some hobbies, but it was when at least Jean and Jerry and I were out of the house. I asked her once if she felt she had given up something. She scoffed at me, saying she wanted to be a mother. I guess that's the answer then. She didn't want to do anything else while we were young but be our mother. Naturally, it was later that she found painting and cross-stitch and building doll houses to fill the time that was no longer needed to care for young children.

Like most children, we had our share of scrapes and bruises. Mom was, by way of her prior training as a nurse, calm and in charge whenever one of us got hurt. As previously mentioned, this included my brother's broken leg, but this was not the limit to our medical care. When I was a preschooler, I was walking with my sister and aunt along the grocery store sidewalk near our house when I tripped and fell into the corner of the window. It was one of those pointed metal window frames, and I cut my face up right next to my right eye. Although I didn't have to go to the hospital, I do distinctly remember being strapped to an examination table while the doctor stitched my face back up. All the while, my mother stood by me, attempting to calm me down. Clearly the situation had me scared, and I was definitely not calm, thus the need for the straps. In first grade, I had my tonsils removed after repeated bouts with sore throats and bronchitis. Unlike now, I spent several days in the hospital, with my mother by my side. Then, my brother went back to Central DuPage Hospital. During high school, he experienced several broken bones, most notably his thumb from playing football. He was way more interested in playing than dealing with his injuries, so these trips to the emergency room usually happened at ten o'clock at night.

The most trips to CDH, however, really goes to my cousin Tim. For several years, whenever Janet Kay would bring her two children, Toni and Tim, up to see us, Tim would wind up in the emergency room. I'm uncertain, but I believe it started with his falling out of the apple tree in our backyard, but it included several stitches and countless x-rays. We counted the trips one Christmas year after Tim had grown up and live through his adventurous but injury prone childhood. I'm pretty sure he was at our hospital six or seven times in about five years. The hospital staff may have wondered if he was being abused, but in fact, he was just the quintessential young boy, afraid of nothing and always willing to get into it. In life's little funny way of dishing out karma, Tim had three boys, all just like him, all with long histories of visiting emergency rooms.

Jan was born in CDH. She being the only child born there in our family. Over the years, like our lives and our family, CDH has grown, evolved, and changed. The stalwart in all of this chaos was always my mother who always remained cool as a cucumber whenever one of us needed that ER. In fact, one night Jerry ended up there, he played most of the football game with a broken thumb. He announced that to my mother as he exited the field. She calmly walked up to me, chatting with my friends, while trying to decide where to go for food, and announced she was taking Jerry to CDH. I, looking stunned, I'm sure, asked if he was ok. She replied that he likely broke his thumb in the second quarter. I asked if she wanted me to go with her and she simply replied, no, just to get home and wait for her to call.

That day I fell into the grocery store window and cut open my face right near my eye. I remember little about that, but what I do remember is being strapped to a table because I wouldn't lie still and my mother's calming voice. Come to think of it, I don't really ever remember my mother being rattled by anything. I didn't really understand this until I too was a mother, faced with a child in crisis and standing in the emergency room watching them be treated. Then I, too, was suddenly cool as a cucumber. At least while I was in the hospital and with my son getting stitches from a dog bite, or my daughter being treated after being thrown from a horse. Late at night, after that child was sleeping soundly, I would tremble with the fear of what might have been and it would hit me, what I might have lost. In the morning, I would be back to my calm self. I wonder if that was how my mother did it? Did she hold it together for us, only to shed the tears of pain and fear out of our earshot and eyesight? Perhaps she was stronger than I am, not needing those private moments to release all the pent-up fear, pain and anger over some moment of crisis. Do we all think our parents are invincible forever, or just until we become parents ourselves?

The whole fam at our last Alzheimer's walk

I'd love to ask her about this, see what she thought that night on the Wheaton Central HS football field, or when I cut my eye. Was she really that calm, or was she just holding it in for us? I can imagine her smiling and laughing at me a little, possibly asking why it matters now, or telling me I'm talking nonsense. Of course, if I ask her today, she probably won't remember these events at all. My telling her about them might make her fearful, like when she sometimes hears us talking about our grandmother that has passed away. It's sad. It's like she just heard it for the first time, and she's upset all over again. Therefore, I probably won't ever know if she was really that calm. I don't want to upset her. That's what we do now. We're careful what we say around her so we don't upset her.

Nineteen

◠◠

The Cigarettes, Being the Blacksheep, and the Telephone

I'm pretty sure my mother started smoking in nurses' training, or possibly just before she graduated from high school. Whenever she started, she was smoking the entire time I was growing up. It sounds bad by today's standards, but remember, this was the early 1960s. She smoked at home, in the car and whenever the family got together. Once, when I was probably eight or nine years old, sitting in our living room, I said to my mother that I wanted to be just like her and smoke like her too. For some reason, this made her mad, and she lit a cigarette and handed it to me. I said no thanks, I would wait until I was older. She insisted I smoke the thing. She instructed me how to suck in on the cigarette and release the smoke. Since it was my mother and I understood you were to obey your parents, I tried it. I then turned green and started coughing and couldn't stop. My mother got me some water, and I even remember her having me stick my head into the frig. Anyway, I still remember the terrible taste of that tobacco and how much I coughed and I have never picked up a cigarette or smoked anything since.

In retrospect, it proved to be a very ingenious plan by my mother to prevent me from smoking. Take away all the mystique of sneaking it, while deciding all on my own not to do it. I was never told I couldn't smoke cigarettes. My mother is brilliant and sneaky!

When I was in high school, Ronald Reagan was President. His wife, Nancy Reagan, worked with the department of education and had commercials on the television and radio to get kids to stop smoking and using drugs. It was the famous, this is your brain on drugs campaign. A person would stand in front of a stove, holding a frying pan. The egg would get cracked and put in the pan. The voice would say this is your brain. Then the frying pan was put on the stove and the egg would cook. The voice would say, this is your brain on drugs. It was very effective. It also made a huge impression on me. I started a campaign of my own to get my mother to stop smoking. It began with retelling the lung revolting experience I had with her and how her lungs must have given up long ago to stop her. Then it became an annoying campaign to just bug her to stop. Finally, in an act of desperation to save my mother from lung cancer, I opened an entire carton of her cigarettes and ran them under the kitchen sink faucet, making them all useless. In my defense, I was trying to give my mother back years of her life. None of my campaigns stopped her. That last one got me grounded for the weekend and forfeiture of my allowance that week to buy a new carton of cigarettes.

While I was in college, she announced she was quitting. We all rejoiced. Until the spring came and I found all the cigarette butts in the gardens, I was told I needed to spend my spring break cleaning out. I confronted her, while no one else was around, and all she could say was that quitting was hard. She tried several more times, each time an issue or event would have her starting back up again. She claimed the cigarettes helped her lose all the weight in the late 1980s. Life has a way of changing things for all of us, and making those hard decisions easier. One winter, while my parents were in Florida for just a few months, the phone rang and my father announced that my mother had been in the emergency room herself. She had a cardiac incident. The doctors thought she had a minor heart attack. Disproven by later tests, but the scare of that night finally convinced my mother to give up the cigarettes. She hasn't smoked since that day. I guess it's true what they say. We each have to decide to give something up in our own time.

Yes, I am the one that thought no one loved me! I couldn't have been more wrong!

If you ask anyone in my family, they will tell you I am the black sheep. I don't believe my transgressions were so great as to warrant that label, but it has stuck with me for most of my life. It is wrapped up with my signature story. While it is true that I have frequently felt my interests and way of doing things have run counter to virtually everyone in my family, I don't know if that makes me the black sheep. Yes, I did prefer books to playing on the field. I drew and painted and sculpted rather than advanced in math classes. Some of my projects took weeks, while others were quick drawings, thus creating all kinds of questions from my father, who didn't seem to understand why other artists at the high school art show had more finished products than I did. All this made me not quite fit in.

The reason might be our birth order. Jean was the oldest, and according to our legendary family stories, the perfectionist who did no wrong. That is definitely not true. I was the middle child, and Jerry was the only boy in the family. Jan is so much younger than all of us that sometimes she seems more like an only child. Anyway, my belief has always been that my label resulted from my being the middle child, sandwiched between the perfect one and the only boy. There is also the fact that during my fifth-grade year of school, I was a very emotional and troubled child, and convinced that no one in my family loved me. Aside from my roller coaster pre-teen emotions, those activities, like football, softball and basketball, were taking up more time inside my family, and perhaps I felt left out.

Whatever the underlying reason, that year I bemoaned my unloved state all the time, and I mean all the time. I plotted running away, made lists of what I would take and on several memorable occasions, I attempted to guilt my mother into admitting my unloved state by revealing to her my plans to leave, and my certainty no one would care. She, as usual, remained calm. She might have even laughed at me, but she told me if that's what I wanted, she would help me pack. This response threw me. Needless to say, I didn't leave home. I often wondered if what I said bothered her or hurt her. I encountered a somewhat similar situation with my daughter many years later and again, while I was in the moment, talking with my daughter, I was calm, just like mom was with me. Later I was upset. I realized then things our children say can hurt us. I really hope I didn't hurt my mother too much with my emotional antics of that year.

What else did I do that warrants this permanent label as the black sheep? Well, during my junior year of high school, I was very busy dating a boy that I thought was way more important than any of the responsibilities I had at home. I also had trouble getting home on time because I just wanted a few more minutes with him. This resulted in at least three rounds of grounding, with escalating consequences and time allotted to the punishment before I learned my lesson. It started at one week, then went to two weeks and then finally to a month with no use of my phone or car except to go to school and work. They grounded me one other time during high school for being a scatter-brain. I went home with a friend and wrote a note to my parents that I was going to sleep over at her house. Then carried the note into my room to answer my phone and left the note under the phone in my room. Left the house, because of course I wrote the note and had a wonderful time with my friend. When she drove me home the next morning, the police were in the driveway. Those parents, you know, the ones that six years prior I was certain didn't love me, had called the police when I didn't come home. I was shaking when I entered the house, not knowing what was going on and certainly not putting all this together as I wrote that note. When I found out the police were there for me, I tried to explain about the note, which my parents said was not there. I went to my room and found the note under the phone. I called my mom into my room to show her. The police left, my parents calmed down, and they grounded me for two weeks. I only needed that lesson once.

So, maybe that's why I'm the black sheep. I'm pretty sure I'm the only one that forced a call to the police. But that's it. I had good grades, on the national honor society, won awards for my artwork. As I've pointed out on these pages, I'm a lot like my mom, except for the smoking thing. She mouthed off to her mother for goodness' sakes and then ran around the yard for twenty minutes, trying to avoid her punishment. Granted, they ground me, not swatted, but we're a lot alike.

As far as I can tell, however, I do not win this black sheep award by much. That sister of mine, the one that is the perfectionist, she has a sordid past as well. She just did all her nonsense before the age of five. My sister once got her hands on a bottle of aspirin and fed some of it to the dog, took a few, and sent the rest down the floor heat duct. Presenting the empty bottle to my mother, they all quickly went to the emergency room (yes, another one of those trips) to have Jean's stomach pumped. Finding only the three aspirin in her stomach, they returned home. The dog was passed out asleep near the floor grate and my father discovered the hoard of aspirin down there. Catastrophe averted. Jean was also a climber. She climbed over and under fences and for one perilous summer was found two, three and four houses away, playing in other people's backyards many times. My parents probably felt they could not take their eyes off of her. All I did was not come home on time, for goodness' sakes. She's at least a very close second in the black sheep competition!

Alas, when we tell the family signature stories, it's mom's flyswatter story, Jean not able to cross Roosevelt Road, my black sheep status and not being loved, Jerry trading his baseball cards for a brother. There are no stories that I can remember for dad or Jan. I wonder why that is?

I grew up during the late 1960s and 1970s. There were no cell phones. We had one house phone. It was torture for me beginning in the sixth grade. I liked to talk on the phone with my friends. We planned our weekend activities on the phone too, which involved multiple calls to a small group of people over and over until we completed all arrangements. My father said that we could only be on the phone for five minutes at a time. This, the source of the torture, was a completely cruel punishment for me. Jean and I researched and presented to our parents the idea that we would get a separate line installed for a phone of our own. After much cajoling and pleading, they agreed. Sweet victory for us! Now I could talk to my friends as long as I wanted, so long as I didn't interrupt Jean's calling activity. In case you haven't figured it out, though, this is the phone that rang that got the note left under it, thus the police visit that fall morning. They also took it away from me during that month long grounding, despite my efforts to explain the injustice of phone I paid for with my money being removed from my room. The rules were the rules. The one thing my mother was always consistent with were the rules. She and my father taught us responsibility and accountability with these rules. By comparison, these periods of punishment were inconsequential when stacked against the importance of the lessons. At the time, they seemed cruel, but just like the cigarette my mother made me smoke, these periods of being grounded for my bad behavior taught me to be responsible. It is these lessons that I thank my mother for. I have, in fact, called her at various times of my adulthood to both thank her for what she's done for me and to apologize. When my kids would act out and I was facing the need to consequence children for their mistakes, I would frequently recall doing those same things to my mother and call to apologize again.

Twenty

The Pharmacy, the Real Estate Agent, and the Dollhouses

My mother returned to work outside of our home when Jan started school. At first it was part time, but once Jan was in school all day, mom went back full time. That first job after nearly two decades of raising kids was at a pharmacy near our home. This pharmacy was like a much smaller version of a Walmart. It had some groceries, some sundries like sewing kits and light bulbs, and small items for your car. There were medicines, first aid items and personal items. It also

Mom behind the counter at the Pharmacy

had cards and wrapping paper, toys, some jewelry, cigarettes, and candy. Oh, and there was a pharmacy counter.

My mother started out as a cashier, then moved to the pharmacy and then ended up dealing with all the cards and wrapping product and ordering, and product placement. She was great in this job for several reasons. First, she was great with people. She could have just about anyone laughing in the few minutes it took to ring up items and was friends to so many that came to the store regularly. She worked hard, managed details and always had an eye for how things should be: should be placed, should be grouped, should be organized. It was just one of her special gifts.

She is why I worked at that same pharmacy during high school and early in college on breaks. I was simply a cashier and stocker, but it paid well by 1980 standards and was close enough to walk to. She worked at that pharmacy for the entire time I was in high school and probably a couple of years of my college days. I think she enjoyed it because it gave her a new sense of accomplishment, something that was kind of her own after years of being someone's mother and I'm sure it was a big deal increasing the household income after years of my father being the only breadwinner. I like that she did this. It seemed to make her happy and gave her something to feel confident and good at.

At some point while she worked at that pharmacy, my mother met the partners of an area builder. They saw in my mother an ability to connect to people and recruited her to work at their model homes in their area developments. She started doing this just on weekends, but one of those weekends she suggested some design changes to a model plan to make it more livable that not only thrilled the customer she was helping, but made a lot of money for the builder. They rewarded my mother by naming a model after her and encouraging her to get her real estate license. She left the pharmacy and went to work for the builder full time. I would come and sit with her on Saturday and Sunday when I came home from college for the weekend. She would meet with foreman, home buyers, tradespeople of all sorts and managed them all. I can remember sitting in the office one Saturday listening to her at the kitchen table, going over design choices with one buyer and the foreman. As I listened, I had a newfound pride in my mother. She was suddenly a different person to me. Not just a mom. She was smart and assertive and strong. That was the day that I understood my example was always my mother. Who I wanted to be like. I don't think I ever told her this story. Certainly, I didn't share with her how much of an inspiration and model she was for me and my sisters. I hate that I can't really tell her now. This disease has robbed me of this chance to tell her how important she has been to my development as a person.

Yes, my mother was kind of a kick (you know what) woman! She sold many houses for that builder. She sold out several of the projects they put her on. When they didn't fulfill some promises they made to her, she became very disillusioned and eventually retired from real estate. When my father retired from teaching, she retired. She was used to having so much occupying her time that she needed a new focus.

At this stage in her life, my mother returned to her creative side. She started building dollhouses. This hobby started out with small kits that were mostly ready to assemble and all parts included. But then it grew into a rather enterprising effort. She sold some, gave some away and then got to a point that she built houses she really wanted and stopped giving them away. In the end, this little hobby had garnered a staggering Christmas colonial, log cabin, beach condo, Victorian cottage, and one, two story something that was not quite finished. There were boxes upon boxes of dollhouses not yet built. There was ready-made furniture of all varieties and kits for furniture to build galore that she scored off of a garage sale one summer for a nominal fee. She had miniature wallpaper, ribbon, accessories like lights and phones and little televisions. Eventually, this little hobby took over an entire room in the basement of their townhouse. It was pretty remarkable. She stained trim and painted exteriors and was almost giddy as she described her latest efforts when we visited.

My daughter, of course, coveted several of these houses when she was younger. So too, my two nieces wanted desperately to play with these marvels of engineering and decoration. These creations were off limits for play. And then the diagnosis came, and over time she spent less and less time working on these houses. I would go into the craft room and look at the partial assembly and look around, saddened by the loss. Losing her interest or ability to work on such a small scale. Losing the vibrant woman who loved to design these houses. In the end, we gave the beach condo to the friends of my parents from high school, now living in Florida. They also got the log cabin, as it closely resembled the lake house in Minnesota those friends had. My granddaughter was the first to be gifted a dollhouse she could play with. My daughter also got the Christmas house she had coveted for many years. The rest I took home to sell for my father to prepare for their permanent move to Florida. In the end, I shipped off all the boxes of houses not yet built and furniture kits and ready-made everything to people across the country. Each time I went to the post office with another box, I marveled at the money I was making for my father, and saddened by this other piece of my mother we were letting go of. On that last day, when I was tasked with ensuring that the townhouse was ready for the walk-through, I went back to that craft room, now completely empty. Standing there for a moment, crying and not knowing why the tears were falling down my face. I guess I was crying at the goodbye to that kick (again; you know what) woman. I don't know why my image of her with those dollhouses was so tied to that day when I knew my mother was so much more than a mother in that model home, but it was, and that empty room felt like I had lost her. It might have been the beginning of my grieving process. That thought that starts slow in your mind when you are caring for an Alzheimer's patient. The thought that says to you, at some point, this disease will take them. It will end their life and you must be prepared. It starts this trickle of the grieving process and the letting go of a person. For me, it started that day, standing in the craft room, that was no more.

Twenty-One

~

White Linen, Cinnabar, and Red Nail Polish

When I was a little girl, I used to marvel at the perfume bottles on my grandmother's dresser. They were so fancy and had tops shaped like all kinds of things, and some even had the little bubble pumps on them to spritz that indelible sent that was Grandma Floye. What I realized some years later is all of those bottles contained the same perfume, Chanel. Whenever I smelled that smell as a child and continuing until today, I think of Grandma and that dresser full of beautiful bottles sitting on the glass tray.

I don't think I noticed my mother's perfume until some years after that first fascination with grandma's. At some point, after my mom went to work at the pharmacy, she discovered Estee Lauder perfume and makeup. They sold Estee Lauder at department stores like Carson's and Marshall Fields, two of the biggest chains in the Chicagoland area. With several fragrances, mom experimented for a few years. She tried Beautiful, and then White Linen. That became her preferred perfume for many years, while she was becoming a real estate agent and spending all those weekends signing contracts and picking features with customers. Because she wore it all the time, I could pick it out in crowds. I would walk through the mall and smell that crisp, floral scent and turn, thinking my mother was nearby.

While I was in college, a new Estee Lauder fragrance came out and that became the scent my mother always wore. Cinnabar is a slightly spicy floral scent and I'm pretty certain my father must have at some point told her he liked it, as it was all she would wear and all we bought for her.

They say that smell is the strongest of your senses. I suppose that's true. Years past, when I would smell pipe tobacco, I would think of my grandfather, and when I smell Chanel, I think of grandma. It will be the same for Cinnabar. When I smell that for the rest of my life, I will be reminded of my mother's dresser, all set up with jewelry boxes and makeup and that bottle of Cinnabar with the red and gold striping.

When my mother started having trouble dressing herself in the morning and someone had to help her, she stopped wearing perfume for a while. Then suddenly, Dad asked for us to buy her some and he started making sure she spritzed it on each morning. It made the scent linger around the house as it had for so many years, and we all appreciated it. I wonder if he wanted this for her to feel more like herself and remember, for him to feel connected to that time in their life or for us. Who knows, but since then, we have helped her dress, helped her brush her hair and her teeth and then sprayed the Cinnabar perfume. Sometimes she would say she liked the smell. Then we would have to explain it was her favorite perfume. I'm glad the memories stay so prominent in my mind, but explaining this to her makes me sad.

Besides perfume, my mother always liked to have her pedicure looking good. She bit her nails badly for a very long time. I did too when I was younger. For those of you with no experience with this, it makes your nails weak for a lifetime. For many years, she had acrylic nails applied so her nails would look nice. At the end of her illustrious career as a real estate agent, she stopped the manicures. However, she continued having pedicures until last summer, when Jean took over the duties.

This might seem a mundane topic, but here's the thing: Mom liked to be fully accessorized, and this was part of it. She liked her nails looking pretty and just about the only color that was acceptable was red. Pink and coral, and bold colors were not acceptable. If I would appear with dark polish on my toenails, she would say she didn't like that. Different shades of red were acceptable. You could have wine, or candy apple, or magenta, but red it was.

I wonder if her adherence to red nail polish was because of its popularity during her coming of age. Perhaps it was daring or the one way she rebelled from her proper dress. We all have those things, don't we, that we hold fast to from our own coming of age? The music you prefer, the favorite article of clothing you can't discard, the style of wearing your hair. For me, it's probably music and shoes. I so much prefer the music of the 1970s and seem to gravitate toward the loafers and pumps so popular when I was graduating from high school.

I've started buying more and more shades of red nail polish recently. When I put something else on, and look down at my toes, I think, hmm, that doesn't look right, and have to redo my nails. I guess mom is right about everything!

And so, we cling to those smells, those somewhat insignificant details of our lives. That makes us who we are, who our family is. Now, we cling to these smells, and that nail polish, to keep her life as normal as we can. Probably as much for us as for her.

Twenty-Two

༄

Grandma's Beach

Her favorite thing to do! Read and soak up
the sun

After my parents were both retired, they began spending time in Florida in the winter months. Starting for a few weeks and then progressively getting longer and longer. They spent one year on the golf coast, but then quickly shifted to spending their snowbird months on the Atlantic Ocean. For most of that time, they were in the same condo on the second floor on the beachfront. We all started visiting them each year on what was our children's spring break. For eight or nine days, we would leave behind the torturous end of winter and drive south loaded down with all kinds of clothes and things, and play on the beach.

The first year we went down there, my youngest son was only five or six years old. He is credited with the label, and we have forever known it as Grandma's beach. Grandma's beach was at the quiet residential end of

Cape Canaveral, Florida. It was about three quarters of a mile from the pier and in the other direction, three quarters of a mile from the port. Every day there were people walking along the waterline, fishing in the surf and laying in the sun. Kids played in the water, tried their hand at the boogie board and the skim boards, and attempted to build sand castles and moats and dig deep, deep holes. We would walk along the beach each day, careful to not disturb any great sand building work, or any scratched in writing we encountered, picking up shells and admiring the kites in the air, and people.

We would get up in the morning and after breakfast, put on our swimming suits, slather sunscreen on every exposed bit of skin and pack up our toys, chairs and towels. We would set up on the beach and lay in the warm sun, watching my mother take the boys out into the water to surf in on their boogie boards. When we got hungry, we would head back up, eat lunch on the balcony, and then reapply the sunscreen before returning to the beach. In the afternoon, we would embark on shell searching and building projects. It was the most relaxing and fun way to spend a day!

One year, there was a tremendous storm out at sea and in the morning, all kinds of shells and especially whole sand dollars had washed up on the beach. We grabbed our bags and walked all the way to the pier, picking on shells. Another year, small jellyfish washed up all up and down the beach. They were purple and looked like squishy balls. Naturally, the boys wanted to poke them with sticks. Some years, the beach eroded to the point there was an enormous drop off down to the water. That year, the building projects included stairs from the high, top part of the beach down to the lower, water level of the beach.

Mom used to take the boys out in the late afternoon with a bag of old bread and they would break it up and feed it to the seagulls and other birds. The birds would swarm around them, flying in circles and looking like a cloud surrounding them. One year, she bought all kinds of kites before we arrived and we spent several days trying to get those into the air, with little success. No matter, the best part of these days was laughing and spending time with mom. She loved the beach. We would sit for hours and read books, laugh at the people on the beach and watch for dolphin and ships coming and going across the water. Naturally, mom was always more tan than any of us, having spent weeks before we arrived sitting on her balcony or patio or down at the beach. I would convey my jealousy and mom would laugh.

We were all sitting there one spring break when this older woman came down to the beach and set up near us. She had a very dark tan, with skin that looked a bit leathery from all the sun. She had a folding chair, and a small cart which she partially emptied. After she set up an umbrella, pulled out a small cooler, I noticed the stack of books in the bottom of that cart. We all whispered about her for a few minutes and then I announced she was what I wanted to be when I grew up. I wanted to be a professional reader at the beach. Mom laughed and said that was a job made for me. We had so much fun on Grandma's beach.

At night, mom and I would sit out on the balcony and watch the water. She once told me that the water calmed her. It's that way for me as well. Hearing the waves and watching the water roll onto the shore and then back out fills me with a sense of peace. When the day has been particularly hard, when caring for mom drains me a little, when she looks at me and doesn't seem to be the mom I always knew, I go back to Grandma's beach, and I stand there for a bit. I remember her sitting in her chair, with her pepsi, reading a book and watching the waves and it provides me some peace of mind. Just as the waves roll into and off of the beach, so do the memories of my mother in my mind.

We don't go to Grandma's beach anymore. Mom and Dad live in a condo on the river side of the outer island so we have to drive to the beach now. When we take mom to the beach, we go to a park that has a bathroom and a walkway over the dune that we can take a wheelchair over. We get mom situated in the wheelchair and take her to just where the sand starts. Then we walk her a short way to where we have the canopy set up and her chair ready for her. We pack lunch and water and some snacks and we sit there and again, watch the waves and people. At some point, mom says she wants to go to the water and we assist her down there and she walks into the water up to her ankles. She looks out over the ocean, thinking who knows what, and then says she wants to go back. We get her back to her chair and she usually smiles. Sometimes she says she likes it there.

Even now, when she can't remember so much, she still, somewhere in there, remembers that she loves the beach. I'm glad we can still do this for her and give her these moments.

Twenty-Three

~

My Father

This story is really about my mother, how she lived, who she was and how she became the woman that is my mother. It is also how Alzheimer's has progressed and robbed us of her. But this story would not be complete without some discussion of my father.

My father is the firstborn of three children, born to parents raised in Missouri. My grandfather worked on the railroad. They lived in a tiny house in Rome, Illinois. It had a well and no indoor plumbing until my father was older and my grandfather was in an accident at work. After months in the hospital with a broken back and a settlement from the railroad, they got indoor plumbing.

In my father's neighborhood, all the boys, regardless of age, played together. Football, baseball, it didn't matter. It made them all very tough. In high school, he played football, basketball and baseball. My father won awards, and more importantly, met and began dating my mother. He graduated from Western Illinois University after being awarded for the highest-grade point average of all athletes in the conference his senior year. He was also then living in the married units with my mother and older sister, Jean, who had been born just before his last year.

My Dad

He spent most of his life working at Lake Park High School. There he was, a math teacher, coach, vice-principal, and finally the principal. He was in charge his whole life, from his siblings, his teammates, his classroom where he taught, on the field and mats of high school sports and, as you might have guessed, in our home. He led our home with the same authority as he led everything else in his life. There were rules and expectations.

Most of the time I remember mom taking care of everything. She would get us up and off to school, make dinner, taxi us to various practices, lessons, and activities. She supervised homework and nursed us through all of our illnesses and injuries. At the end of each summer, she would gather us all up and walk through the department store, buying all the items we needed for the new school year. My father was busy working through all this. Despite that, we ate dinner together nearly every night. He would come in just as the dinner preparation was getting finished and we would sit down. He would ask about our days and then engage Jerry in sport discussions the rest of the meal. Then he would get into his sport shorts and t-shirt and sit in his big chair with the ottoman and watch television. He talked little and sometimes fell asleep sitting in that chair.

My dad would get involved if one of us had homework we couldn't figure out. When we had misbehaved, or later when decisions centered on when we needed to be home from a night out, he was the guy. He doled out allowance and chores. It was my father who grounded me when I failed to come home on time and he was the one that removed my phone from my room when I failed to learn the lesson after two other attempts. I would have to say that I felt closer to my mother all that time than to my father. He seemed this quiet force in our house that was not to be messed with.

It always seemed to me that dad had way more in common with my brother than with his daughters, or maybe just me. I was more into reading and art than sports. I was an average math student, except for geometry. That class really threw me and it was the first and only time I got a "C" in high school. Consequently, my father and I talked very little while I was younger. When I was older, and in college, it was my mother I would call to check in with. Even into adulthood, it was my mother I spent time with and called with updates about my kids and activities. I guess you could say I was a little in awe and maybe fear of him. Which is funny, because I never felt afraid at home, with that exceptional time when I was convinced no one loved me!

There are a few exceptions to this that give a glimmer of who my father really is. When I was in high school, he was the one that took me to the mall to view my awarded artwork on display. We had to walk through all the art and he asked me questions until we came to my drawing. We stood there for a long time. The interesting thing was he had to go. I don't know if he cancelled some other commitment to be there, but he spent the entire morning with me that day.

When I was a freshman in college, he was the one that took me to the appointments when I had to have my wisdom teeth pulled. He took a day off work to do this. To be clear, I think my father took maybe eight or nine days off work the entire time he was working at Lake Park. Several days, probably a week's worth, were for my grandfather's funeral when I was in third grade. I remember he was home the day Jerry had to have his thumb re-broken after a high school football game and late-night ER trip to reset it correctly. And this day to take me to have my wisdom teeth pulled.

Clearly, my father was a quiet man, but there was always an inkling of something more. The birth of the first grandchild changed all of this. He became warm and playful with the grandkids and, I might add, a much more patient helper with homework than he seemed when I was struggling with geometry. At some point, he became warmer with all of us and started hugging as we gathered and left from each other's homes.

One of the greatest gifts my father gave me was shortly after I separated from my first husband. I called him and told him I thought my son was struggling with the separation and I could not seem to get through to him. My father stepped in. He talked with him, took him places, spent time with him. He became the strong male role model for my son. I will never forget how he kept my young boy from falling during that time. That son is an adult now, and he still talks about how his grandfather helped him through eighth grade.

Then my mother was diagnosed with Alzheimer's, and everything changed. At first it seemed like dad didn't want to admit there was a problem, but really, I came to realize that he was facing an insurmountable battle and was simply trying to prepare. He was doing what had always come naturally to him; assess the problem, find the solutions, and execute. As mom got worse, we could all tell that his priority shifted to singularly focused on mom. Things that would have bothered him a few years before were no longer important. In fact, at one point, when one of the beloved grandchildren behaved badly on a phone call and ended it by calling his grandfather a terrible name, he reacted totally out of character. What some years ago would have resulted in a family sort of meeting where my father took this young man to task was now met with silence. He simply did not have time for such nonsense when the love of his life needed him.

Over time, as my mother needed more and more help to do anything, my father provided all she needed. He did their laundry, bought the groceries, helped her dress, made her meals, and took her to appointments. Through all that he cared that she still got out of the house for dinner as she was able, met the family for Sunday breakfasts, and continued to get her pedicures. As I watched this, my long-held belief of who the caregiver in our family was changed. I would watch in wonder as my father helped her put on jewelry and perfume and get her shoes on.

Now, this is not to say that the leader of my childhood was no longer there at all. Sometimes he would get frustrated with my mom. When she refused to get up from her chair to get ready for dinner, he would argue with her, as she continually simply said "No." He would finish his dinner and then bring her dinner to her chair. He would also get frustrated when she suddenly couldn't do something that yesterday she could do with little direction, or when he had to explain for the five hundredth time how to put her shoes on. Somewhere in each of these incidents, I'm sure he would stop himself and remind himself he needed to show patience and he would walk away for a minute and go back to her and show her again.

Despite these frustrating incidents, each time they walked from the car to the doctor's office, or from the car to the restaurant, she would reach for his hand and they would hold hands. Every single time. I don't know if that was mom reaching for him, knowing he was her safe place or dad trying to reassure her or himself. I just know that this holding of hands has been the symbol of their devotion to one another. It might also be the reason I think everything will be ok, even when I know it won't.

Dad has had a struggle, clearly, to be the primary caregiver for an Alzheimer's patient. He has had to recognize his own limitations, that he cannot do this all by himself and, occasionally, actually ask for help. There have been moments when I have been overcome with sadness thinking about how this is impacting my father. The girl he fell in love with, married, laughed with, had children with, was drifting away. The overwhelming grief he must experience daily brings tears to my eyes. When the tears subside, I am in awe of him. The strength he must have, the devotion to her, the love he shows her every day, is inspiring and daunting.

I don't know how my siblings feel, but I see my father in a whole new way now. He has always been strong; he has always put his family first, and he has always done everything in his power to help his children. It's different now. He has shown his love for my mother in so many ways, ways we either didn't notice or weren't around to see all those years. As terrible as this disease has been for my mother and our family, I know it has blessed me to witness this love between my parents.

The interesting thing is that after all these years when I didn't feel I had anything in common with my father, now I seem to find some common ground. I call and talk to him; I confide things to him, and we have subjects we can discuss. Who knew all the years when all that was talked about at our table was sports that my father had an interest in other things? It is sad though, that as I am losing my mother, I am finding my father. I wish I had a chance to go back and do some things differently. I wish I could have this wisdom and this better relationship with my father, without my mother having to have Alzheimer's.

Twenty-Four

~

How We Manage Now, the Role Reversal, and the Emptiness

Everything changed after that diagnosis, and has continued to change as the years passed. First, we had to plan to ensure she wasn't alone for long periods of time. She stopped driving shortly after dad had to provide her very explicit directions to meet friends, but still she had trouble finding her way home. She even candidly admitted this to my aunt Janet Kay, saying that she probably shouldn't drive anymore. So, she had to be driven everywhere. Then we had to put labels on all the drawers, cabinet and shelves so she could find everything and put items back so that we could find them later. Then she couldn't be left alone at all. That was a big change. We had to get serious then. Calendars had to be compared and one of us had to be at the house whenever dad had to go anywhere. For a while, we had to have notes on all the sliding doors to the balcony and the front door to keep my mother from going out of the house without someone with her. Eventually, we installed another lock on the front door so she couldn't open it by herself.

Mom with her great granddaughter

It got very real one fall day when my father called us all to say he had been in a car accident. He had gone to run a quick errand and someone had pulled out around a car waiting to turn left and t-boned my father's car. He was there for a long time and the police officer drove him home because his car was no longer drivable. Of course, we all went directly to their house to see him to verify for ourselves he was ok. During the next few days, we helped him settle with the insurance company and get a new car. At the same time, I was contemplating what would have happened if that accident had been worse. What if he was really hurt and taken away in an ambulance? My mother didn't answer the phone or the door anymore. When would we hear this had happened? What if mom had gone outside looking for him after hours sitting there alone and walked far enough from their house and she couldn't find her way home? That was the last day mom was left alone for dad to do anything. If he left, someone was with her.

After that fateful day when mom was hospitalized, we settled into the "new normal". One of us was at mom and dad's house each day in the afternoon to help. Dad could run errands then, or take care of appointment scheduling and bills or maybe even catch a nap, while one of us got mom lunch and sat with her. If dad had a doctor's appointment, one of us would go with dad and one would stay with mom.

Whenever mom's medical situation worsened, like that hospitalization, our schedule only adjusted so that one of us was with dad all day. These periods usually lasted for about a week and then we would go back to the regular afternoon plans. Eventually, as we learned, Alzheimer's patients don't fully get back to normal. They plateau at a new normal until the next issue. So over time, mom simply required more attention. However, spending the afternoon with them meant making sure she ate lunch and sometimes helping with her shower and assisting her to the bathroom.

During outings, like to breakfast on Sunday and when we took mom out for dinner, there were additional needs for my mother's care. Someone had to keep a Kleenex handy because, for some reason, every time my mother ate food, her nose ran. If she had to use the restroom, someone had to accompany her, partly to assist, and partly to ensure she made it back to the table.

This is how we manage now. Helping her get out of her chair, helping her eat, helping her dress, and brush her teeth. It's an amazing role reversal. Where she had cared for us when we were young children and didn't know how to brush our teeth or cut up our food, now we did that for her. There were times when this seemed strange. This was that invincible mother I knew, the one that can no longer shower on her own. In the beginning, she only wanted my father to help her in the bathroom, but at some point, she didn't seem to care. Almost like she'd lost the ability to be embarrassed.

Talking with her or asking her even a simple question became difficult. She more often than not simply repeated the question. "Do you want grilled cheese or turkey for lunch?" would get that question back. The interesting thing, and perhaps something we should all be thankful for, is that she forgot how to do so many things, but she still remembered who we were and who dad was.

However, there is an emptiness to this role reversal. Yes, we all gladly help our father provide care for our mother, but sometimes I just wish my mom would look at me and laugh like she used to. The moments when I would look at her and see that woman, the girl that broke the bed and climbed over barbed wire fences had become very infrequent. We get so focused on the day-to-day care that we seem to miss that we are already grieving for her. Late at night, after I've been over there helping, I realize I miss the days when she would admonish us for misplacing something. She had really put it somewhere else and we couldn't find it, but at least then my mom was my mom.

There is such a sadness to this realization that your parent is slipping away. That she is behaving more like a child than the parent now. I still try to engage her. Occasionally saying outrageous things, hoping she will laugh like she used or admonish me. I miss those days from just a year ago when she constantly wanted to call me to her chair while I was making something in the kitchen to hold my hand. She would grasp it and squeeze it. I would tell her she was holding me too tight and she would smile at me. I miss those days already.

The whole fam at Sunday breakfast

Still, we find things to celebrate. When we tell her it's time for dinner and walk over to her sitting in her chair and say we need to get up and go to the table and she just remembers how to stand up from a chair and does that. We all cheer. When we've had to go to several appointments and she has to get into and out of the car and one of those times she turns, puts her feet out on the ground, holds onto the car door frame and stands up, I do the happy dance because she remembered. She smiles when we make a big deal out of these small accomplishments. I don't know if she understands why we're cheering, but she likes it when we do this. It might seem strange the way we make a big deal out of standing up or getting out of the car, or remembering who the people in a picture are, but these are things we celebrate now with our mother.

I find you have to cheer about even these small things. When she remembers how to get up or sit down in a car, or says something funny after not saying anything all afternoon. You have to find things to be cheerful about to keep that sadness at bay.

The one event that she seemed to understand recently was my parents' anniversary. When the cards arrived, she would read them and look over, smiling at dad. We took them to dinner. She understood when we said we were celebrating their marriage. I was very thankful that night.

My parents have some friends from high school that live nearby, Doug and Karen. They were good friends and remained good friends their whole lives. Karen has Alzheimer's too. She was recently placed in a memory care facility because her care requirements had become too great for home. She also was forgetting who her husband was and frequently tried to leave their home. It broke my heart when I heard about this. A year ago, we borrowed a wheelchair from Doug. He met us near his garage to get it out and helped Rich put it in our trunk. Doug looked exhausted as he told us he couldn't hardly even shower for fear of what she would do. We drove away from his house and I said to Rich that I was sorry, but I was thankful that my mother forgot how to brush her teeth and not who my father was. I cannot imagine the pain that would cause the person not suffering from this terrible disease to look into the eyes of someone they married decades ago and realize they didn't know you anymore. Doug and Karen are good friends, but for just that moment, I was glad that wasn't happening to my mother.

Alzheimer's is a tricky disease. One person may be fine for decades while another one loses everything quickly. One may forget skills like brushing teeth or hair or how to hold silverware, while another may forget everyone in their family. That was always my fear. I was always fearful that I would walk up to my mother, sitting in her chair, and she wouldn't know who I was. It's trying and an exercise in patience to help my mother get dressed and put shoes on, but I am oh so thankful she remembers who we are.

So, everything about our family is different now. What we celebrate, what we stress over and focus on, and how we look at the world. That's what Alzheimer's does. It steals from you and it changes everyone it touches.

Twenty-Five

~

Losing Mom

Starting in December, my mother had one issue after another. First, it was another UTI, then it was a head cold, then she had to get the Covid booster shot. We called the doctor and said we believed she had a UTI. We tested her at home and we started her on antibiotics. The doctor ordered the lab test as they couldn't trust that home test we did. Three days after she started stumbling again, and tested at home and started the meds, the lab found no UTI. Dad continued to give her the antibiotic, anyway. We let that run its course, and she got better and could walk without someone holding both her hands and someone walking behind to keep her stable.

A week later, she started coughing. Her nose ran even when she wasn't eating and as these colds do, it settled in her chest. She was breathing harder and shorter. So, we called the doctor again. We started her on a zpac this time. We also got out the nebulizer so we could get medicine into her lungs to clear out the fluid that had collected there. She got better. Not totally back to what we considered normal, but better.

Dad had recommendations from the doctor for them both to get the booster shot, so when mom was doing better, he took her in for these shots. She had an awful weekend after that shot. She was confused, and couldn't communicate very well and again had trouble walking.

Her breathing wasn't totally better, so we kept doing the nebulizer. I noticed a milky sort of mucus on her mouth in the morning when she was helped out of bed and commented to dad that it might indicate that she had thrush, which was common with prolonged use of the nebulizer when you don't rinse your mouth out after the treatment. Getting mom to rinse her mouth out was beyond her scope of understanding at this point, so we simply made her drink water after the treatment.

It had bothered me that each time mom had an issue; we seemed to be better at noticing it, but we had trouble gathering the medical resources to act on it quickly enough. Fortunately, mom had a regular appointment on Tuesday of that week with her neurologist. We learned a few things during that visit. First, we talked about the lack of access to medical personnel when mom started having issues. The doctor said he could approve a home care nurse that would come in once a week and check on mom and would have the ability to get in touch with doctors. I was excited about this. Second, he explained the "step" nature of Alzheimer's to us. Each time an Alzheimer's patient has other, seemingly unrelated health issues, like that cold and UTI, the brain functions react to help the body handle that, which causes the degradation of the Alzheimer's symptoms. Treating the outside issue will allow the patient to recover a bit, but never get back to their original starting point, thus creating this stair step effect. This happens in the later stages of Alzheimer's. The doctor also told us that because of this step effect, treatment of issues coming in quick succession, like my mother was experiencing, requires more and different treatments. Great. That means no more zpac when she gets bronchial colds. He also examined the white milky substance and said it was not thrush, but severe dehydration. I didn't know this reaction indicated dehydration, so I learned several things that day.

The doctor instructed us to push fluids and if she didn't improve quickly, to take her to the emergency room for IV fluid intervention. He also said he would order a chest x-ray and bloodwork for the next day to ensure she didn't have any residual infections and we went home. We pushed fluids as much as possible Tuesday evening, but Wednesday, we didn't get as much fluid into her as we hoped. Having the labs and chest x-ray meant mom was at the lab unit of the hospital for several hours, without drinking much. Wednesday evening, I was called by my dad because mom wasn't drinking enough and he and Jan were worried. I agreed, and we left for the emergency room.

Thankfully, by this time, more than the patient was allowed in the examining room. Covid had receded enough that both my dad and I were allowed into the ER unit. For the first hour, we refused several tests and repeatedly asked for IV fluids, per the recommendations of my mother's doctor. We would not allow them to covid test my mother. But we refused a chest x-ray (in case you've not connected these dots, we had one of those that morning at that same hospital), and then we refused an MRI. In all that time, we saw two nurses and two different lab technicians, but not an attending doctor. My mother finally got her IV of fluids and miraculously started talking again and laughing at the doctors. She even told the doctor "This is bulls***!" when I said we didn't need an MRI, we already knew our mother had Alzheimer's. However, the doctor and the nurses, aggravated with our refusal to do all these tests, simply discharged my mother after the one bag of IV fluids and sent us home. They didn't review the bloodwork that had been completed that morning, or discuss it with us. Although it ended with mom communicating a bit again, at one point she focused on the corner of the room and kept saying "Mom, mom, mom." I asked her who she was talking to, and she said her mother was there. It frightened me. I got mom's attention and tried to talk to her for a few minutes until my father returned. I never told him about this. It was a foreboding I didn't understand yet.

Thursday was not my day to help dad, per our scheduling, but I checked with my sister and mom seemed to accept fluids. We got two Gatorade bottles and about 30 ounces of water down her. Hopeful the dehydration was being addressed; I went over to help my dad on Friday morning. We woke mom up at about 10am. That milky stuff was dripping down the side of her face and onto her pajamas, but it was a kind of yellow now. I mentioned it to my father as we prepared to help her out of bed. She was very sluggish and hard to fully wake up, but I figured she had been through a lot this week and dismissed it. We got her into the bathroom and had her sitting on the toilet when I turned to get the wipes to clean her up and turned back and her head had lolled over to her left side. I was alarmed and got dad's attention. We tried to wake her and could not. I ran for the phone to call 911. I reached the 911 operator and told them my mother wasn't breathing. The 911 operator instructed us to get her flat on the floor and administer chest compressions. I started, but dad clearly wanted to do this, so I turned that over to him and went out and propped the door open for the emergency people and ran back and forth until they arrived.

I went back to dad and asked if he needed me to take over. Of course, he didn't. I searched for a pulse and couldn't find it and tried to give her mouth-to-mouth. Then I heard the emergency people, and I ran back to direct them to where we were. Three paramedics, a fireman and two sheriffs came into the house carrying all kinds of bags. The two sheriffs pulled my dad and I out of the bathroom and into the living room. They got both my and dad's information. Two more firemen came in with a stretcher and the sheriff directed us to the back of the house, into dad's office. I kept asking how mom was and finally the sheriff went to check on the status. She came back and told us they were trying to stabilize mom for the trip to the hospital but they had her heart beating. The sheriff asked if there was anyone we needed to call and Dad told me to call Jean and Jan and Jerry. I started with Jean and she left immediately to come over. Jan said she was meeting us at the hospital. Jerry said he would start looking at flights.

Through all of this, I know I was crying and breathing hard, but it seemed like I was calm enough, because I talked to the sheriff and made the calls. Dad was crying and trembling. When they had mom out, they let us come out. I said my phone and glasses were back in that bathroom and someone went to get them as they were still cleaning up. Then dad and I left for the hospital. We neglected to call Jean back to tell her we had left, so she went first to their house before coming to the hospital. When we got to the hospital, the intake nurse took us to a small room off the hallway and Jan was there. Jean arrived, the nurse brought us water, and then we waited for what seemed like an eternity. It was probably only about 30 minutes. I could tell dad was getting agitated, so I went out and asked the intake nurse if there was any possibility that dad could go be with mom. She said she would check.

About two minutes later, two doctors came into the room we were waiting in and shut the door. I knew before they even started talking. They explained that had resuscitated her at their house, in the ambulance, and twice in the emergency room, but they could not stabilize her. She was gone. I folded in half and reached out for Jean, sitting to my right and dad, sitting to my left. I think the doctors kept talking, but I heard nothing. The next thing I remember was that intake nurse asking if we wanted to see her. Dad said yes and stood up. We stood and followed, but let him lead. He went into this room filled with machines and monitors and lay down across mom and just cried over and over, "No, no, no." He kissed her, and then he motioned for us to get closer to her. We each took turns holding her hand and kissing her. Several times dad went back to kiss her again and cry again, "No, no, no."

A nurse came in and said when we were ready, he had some questions and information for us. We went out. He wanted to know where she would go after the medical examiner gave his ruling. That's when I seemed to calm down. I called my aunt Linda, told her what happened and asked for the funeral home in Chillicothe. She text me the number after we talked and spread the word. I called the funeral home, and the funeral director graciously took all the details in hand. He called the hospital and got a funeral home to receive her and prepare her to travel up to Chillicothe, as that was where my mother and father wanted to be laid to rest. While that funeral director took charge, I called my kids, Rich, and we called Jerry back. Then we left the hospital and went back to dad's house. Yes, it was dad's house now. As empty as I felt with my mother being so needy and so not the woman she had been my whole life, this was a new emptiness, a deeper, darker emptiness. Things would never be the same. From January 28, 2022, our lives would never be the same.

The next week was a blur. We picked clothes for my mother, cleaned her jewelry dad wanted her to be wearing, picked the casket, the flowers and made all the arrangements. We would not have been able to do all this without the help of our cousin Toni and dad's sister Janet. They found a minister, checked on flowers, called people, and made the lunch arrangements for us. We went through just about every picture in the house, and Jan made these beautiful canvas picture collages of my mother's life. Will all the calls made, and all the preparations taken care of, we planned our trip north to bury my mother.

Naturally, because we had to travel north, mother nature helped us by sending a huge snow and ice storm across the middle of the country for us to drive through. The bad weather hit just after we crossed the river into Illinois. First it was ice, then on top of that ice it was snow. It was a treacherous day. All along the drive, I was checking in with the funeral director to ensure that my mother was being prepared and sent on a plane to Illinois as well. With all that weather, it was a stressful trip on many levels.

What I remember about that day was not the cold, and it was freezing. Not that all of us from Florida didn't have winter coats, and we had to borrow from family to stay warm that day. What I remember was the throng of people that came to say goodbye to my mother. Friends I didn't know about, people she went to school with, even her high school gym teacher. Family from Missouri drove over despite the weather. Mr. Monken made the trip with his son Ted, despite his suffering from Parkinson's disease. Mrs. Monken didn't come. She had suffered a stroke that left her incapable of traveling. I remember how painful and yet how comforting it was to have my son hold me when I fell apart in front of her casket. I remember how each time I fell apart, Rich was instantly at my side. And I remember the way all of my mother's grandchildren gathered at one table at lunch and talked about all their memories of her. Most of all, I remember the pain I felt as I walked away from that closed casket, walked back to our car on the freezing bitter February day, away from my mother forever.

At some point, Jean mentioned she was glad it was me that was there that day. She said she would not have been able to be calm enough to make the call and help dad. I look back on it and I don't think I was very calm, but maybe. Maybe I had that same calmness that mom had when a crisis was going on. Maybe I held it together, just like she did when I was sick or hurt.

When we got back to Florida, the first thing I did was go to the beach. Not just any beach, but Grandma's Beach. I stood there, by the water's edge, watching the waves rush onto the shore and asked the wind if she was there. This place she loved, surely, she would be there, and I would feel her again. The wind changed a bit. I sat there for a long time, watching the waves and thinking of the days we would sit there, reading, laughing at people walking by and soaking up the sun. I wasn't sure it would ever be fun again to sit at the beach. All I would do was think of how she loved it and how she was missing it. I walked back to my car and as I came off the boardwalk that crossed the dune, a cardinal flew a few feet in front of me into the bushes. It flew out across me again as I walked to my car, and then turned over the drive and fly again, just in front me. Yes, she was there. That is all we have of her now. That and our memories of her. I smiled for the first time in a week, but the sadness didn't seem to dissipate.

Twenty-Six

~

Reflections

We stayed with my aunt, Janet Kay, during the few days we were in Chillicothe for my mother's funeral. She was a tremendous help to me. I guess at that point I wanted to hear about my mother. I wanted to learn more about her and just needed to talk after a week of planning. Janet must have wanted to talk, too. We talked for hours and it was an incredible comfort to me. It was also very enlightening.

For most of my life, my mother acted like and often spoke of the difficult relationship she had with her mother-in-law, my father's mother. This seemed more than plausible to me as I always knew Nany, as we call her, doted on her first-born son, my father. It might not have mattered who my father married to Nany in some respects. Now, my mother was always pleasant with Nany, but she would mention to me on some drives to Chillicothe that Nany didn't like her. So, I spent my whole life believing there was no love lost between my mother and my grandmother. Janet Kay told me things that totally changed that belief.

Janet Kay detailed many situations and circumstances where, in fact, Nany had told Janet Kay to call Lee to get advice. Janet even said that Nany really admired and loved my mother. This was big news. As I sat in her living room, trying to stay warm during the coldest February in years, awaiting the funeral and burial of my mother, I was incredulous. How could my mother never have known the level of admiration that Janet Kay was describing Nany having for her? It saddened me in a way that no other part of the previous week had, surprisingly. I was sad that my mother didn't know that her mother-in-law thought the world of her. It was in that moment the genuine sense of loss settled into my heart. All the things she wouldn't know, wouldn't see, wouldn't hear, wouldn't get to enjoy. How would we ever know how to feel in these days without her?

Just as my father had cried "No, no, no" in the hospital, I spent the entire day of the funeral screaming that at the top of lungs inside my head. No, this could not be happening. That was not my mother laying in that coffin, this simply was not happening. Each time I looked over at her, I fell apart.

But, as it has since the beginning of time, life goes on. We returned home and contemplated life without her. My sisters and I still plan each week on who will cover which days, but now it is to ensure that our father goes on, finds his way, for the first time in his life, living alone. As time passed, and the business of a person's end is dealt with, we went through her things. One of these days, Jean said to me in a moment we were alone, "I'm so glad it was you that was there that day. I don't think Jan or I would have been as calm as you were." It surprised me. Later that night, when I again couldn't sleep for thinking of my mother, I contemplated what Jean had said. I certainly didn't feel all that calm the day we lost her, but maybe I appeared that way to others. Was that my mother's guiding hand, knowing that there had to be someone in that day that was calm and collected? I'd like to think so. But, in fact, that day, it was not my mother's voice I heard, but my grandmother's. As I ran from the bathroom to the front door to direct the emergency workers to where my mother was lying on the bathroom floor, I distinctly heard my grandmother say, "It's ok, Lee. Everything's going to be ok." Then as I was being shooed out of the bathroom by the Sheriff, I heard her again, but talking directly to me as if from another room say, "Joy, just go in the other room, It's ok, I'm here." I've told no one about this. But it was my grandma that calmed me down that day. Perhaps I imagined it, but it has been a source of peace for me since that day. The thought of my mother being guided from her life by her mother makes some of this better. Upon reflection, I remember my mother laying in the emergency room, calling her mother. My father was out of the room and it scared me. But now, was my grandmother there? Were my mother's systems starting to shut down that Wednesday evening?

I spent many nights going over everything. Everything we did in those last days, everything I did that last day. I've cried many nights over the loss of my mother. Each day I try to collect my thoughts about her, about her disease and how we cared for her.

Here are a few things I've learned since January. First, Nany really admired my mother. Lots of others really liked my mother. They were at the funeral, and later at a luncheon when we returned for the placing of the stone at the cemetery. The ladies regaled us with stories of their escapades. There was a trip to the water tower and allegedly an attempt to climb said tower, that I had not heard about despite my calls for information for this book from them a year ago, and some vague winter weekend sleepover event where alcohol was secreted to a nearby snow drift for safekeeping. I have found that I am profoundly jealous when I see an older person who is totally functioning fine, especially if they are with family. I hope that goes away. I hope I can learn to rejoice in other's good health and family gatherings.

We suddenly, after several months, found several old photo albums of trips my parents made that seemed like a treasured discovery, seeing my mother in places she visited and the fun she had. These stories and pictures further detail the fun, feisty young woman, mother, wife and friend that was my mother.

I've also learned a lot more about Alzheimer's since my mother's death. First, and something I find appalling, there are very few tests to diagnose and thus treat early. Most tests involve a very subjective cognitive assessment, which is a series of conversationally delivered questions. However, there are starting to be advancements in testing related to proteins called amyloid-beta that are a hallmark of Alzheimer's. There is an awakening of awareness as to the impact of medicine and procedures on Alzheimer's patients, like regular old ordinary anesthetics and some statin drugs. The other interesting thing I've learned is that studies are showing medical grade CBD seems to do some remarkable things with Alzheimer's patients in early stages, even to the point of reversal. Anyone reading this, that is involved in the care of an early-stage Alzheimer's patient, should look into this. Of course, these studies are all going on overseas, and as a treatment, are not supported or sanctioned by the powers that be in the United States. I think the message here is research. Don't just take anyone's word for it. Ask the questions, bug the doctors and nurses, and get the resources you need.

I've learned so much about my mother and her life. How she played and laughed and was loved by her family and friends. She has become so much more than a mother. You might say I've idolized her now, now that she's gone, I've glossed over her mistakes and her personality flaws. I don't believe that's true. Here are some things about my mom that I didn't talk about. She hated cats. She didn't enjoy eating salad, at least in the last few years. Watching people and criticizing their clothing and actions was something my mother enjoyed doing, even as it was not particularly kind. Most of her life, she really didn't like getting her face wet. She would not dunk her head into pools, even our own. This also presented all kinds of problems when we had to help her shower. You had to have an extra towel for her to hold over her eyes to keep from getting water in her face. So she was not perfect.

The truth is, she was a good woman. She was funny; she had great, lifelong friends. She was a devoted wife and mother. She was a successful nurse, cashier and real estate agent.

As I reflect on my mother's life, her disease, and what I hope others take from this, I find it boils down to this. No matter how average a person's life is, there is remarkable in there as well. My mother didn't make headlines. My mother was not a millionaire or famous for anything. She was an average girl growing up in a small town in central Illinois. Meeting and falling in love with her husband as a freshman in high school, she loved her family. She got in trouble, she laughed; she made clothes, dollhouses and loved the beach. My mom raised four children, had eight grandchildren, and one great-grandchild. She had an ordinary life, but an extraordinary one.

How I want to remember her

JB Yanni, a beach lover, and shoe collecting offspring of her superhero mother. Surrounded by a boisterous, but fun and loving family, she began writing while still a teen on school newspapers and the yearbook. Always searching for creative outlets, she painted, drew and sculpted before finding her way to writing novels.

Although generally a fiction novelist, this book represents a very personal journey of discovery of who her mother was, what she left to her family and friends and how Alzheimer's effects people.

A great collector of all manner of books, JB believes a book can change you and move you and become a lifelong friend. When not writing, you can find JB with a book or Kindle in her hand. Her motto: In my utopia, books are free and reading makes you thin!

Other works by JB include the Time Benders series of time travel adventures. Available on Amazon and other online retailers. You can see what else JB is writing at her website: jbyanni.com, and can catch her on Facebook at jb_yanni and on twitter @jb_yanni.